Investing with She's *on the* M●ney

Victoria Devine is a multi-award-winning financial adviser who is transforming the way millennials think about money.

With a background in behavioural psychology, her own financial advisory business, Zella, and a chart-topping podcast, Victoria understands what makes her generation tick and she knows how to make hard-to-understand concepts fun, fresh and relatable.

Victoria has been a guest speaker at events and featured in publications such as the *Financial Standard*, *Vogue*, Business Chicks 9 to Thrive, ABC News, RMIT Future of Financial Planning, Mamamia, *Elle* magazine, Yahoo Finance and many more. She has also been named on the *Forbes* 30 Under 30 Asia list for 2021.

Victoria's number one bestselling first book, *She's on the Money*, won the ABIA General Non-fiction Book of the Year 2022 and the Best Personal Finance & Investment Book of the Year at the 2021 Business Book Awards.

If you can't find her, chances are she's at home with an oat latte in one hand and her Old English Sheepadoodle, Lucy, in the other.

shesonthemoney.com.au

@shesonthemoneyaus

@ShesontheMoneyAUS

Also by Victoria Devine

She's on the Money

Investing with She's *on the* Money

Build your future wealth

Victoria Devine

PENGUIN LIFE

UK | USA | Canada | Ireland | Australia
India | New Zealand | South Africa | China

Penguin Life is part of the Penguin Random House group of companies
whose addresses can be found at global.penguinrandomhouse.com

Penguin
Random House
Australia

First published by Penguin Life in 2022
Copyright © Victoria Devine 2022

The moral right of the author has been asserted.

Cover and text design by Alissa Dinallo © Penguin Random House Australia Pty Ltd
Illustrations by Louisa Maggio © Penguin Random House Australia Pty Ltd

Author photograph by Miranda Stokkel

Typeset in 10.5/14 pt Mercury Text by Post Pre-press Group, Australia

Graph on p. 80 reprinted with permission © Vanguard Australia Investments Ltd, 2022.
See p. 285 for disclosure. Graph on p. 112 reprinted with permission © McCrindle.

At the time of publication, Victoria Devine is a Corporate Authorised Representative
(No.1295105) of Infocus Securities Australia Pty Ltd ABN 47 097 797 049 AFSL
No. 236523, a wholly owned subsidiary of Infocus Wealth Management Ltd.

Printed and bound in Australia by Griffin Press, an accredited
ISO AS/NZS 14001 Environmental Management Systems printer

A catalogue record for this
book is available from the
National Library of Australia

ISBN 978 0 14377 876 9

penguin.com.au

MIX
Paper from
responsible sources
FSC® C009448

We at Penguin Random House Australia acknowledge that Aboriginal and Torres
Strait Islander peoples are the Traditional Custodians and the first storytellers
of the lands on which we live and work. We honour Aboriginal and Torres
Strait Islander peoples' continuous connection to Country, waters, skies and
communities. We celebrate Aboriginal and Torres Strait Islander stories, traditions
and living cultures; and we pay our respects to Elders past and present.

**The information in this book is of a general nature only and does not take into
account your financial situation, objectives or needs. The information has been
compiled from sources considered to be reliable at the time of publication, but
not guaranteed. Before acting on any of this information, you should consider
its appropriateness to your own financial situation, objectives and needs.**

As the author of this book I'd like to acknowledge and pay respect to Australia's Aboriginal and Torres Strait Islander peoples, the traditional custodians of lands, waterways and skies across Australia. I'd like to particularly acknowledge the Wurundjeri people of the Kulin Nation who are the traditional custodians of the land on which I was able to write this book. I pay my respects to Elders past and present, and I share my friendship and kindness.

For you.

I'm so proud of you and how far you've come,
and even prouder that you're putting Future You first.

Contents

Prologue

When I sat down to write my first book, I was on a mission to empower my wonderful community – and everyone else I could possibly reach – on their financial journeys. There were so many ways I wanted to help people with *She's on the Money* – hopefully the fact you're reading this means it helped you and you are keen to learn more about how you can achieve financial freedom!

Since *She's on the Money* was released and landed on bookshelves across the country, I've been absolutely blown away by the response. Every other day I hear from someone who has read the book and put their learnings into action. It genuinely is a 'pinch me' moment to realise that I've played a part in helping people to get their financial ducks in a row, make educated money decisions and ultimately move forwards on the path towards building wealth.

Now, you might be wondering why I wanted to write this new book on investing. Well, while my first book was a general guide to all things personal finance, with this book I want to delve further into the exciting world of investing. And, I promise you – it *is* an exciting world!

Investing is a fundamental tool for building your future wealth, and in this book I'll let you in on why. For sure, investing can be scary or intimidating if you're not familiar with it – and there's no doubt that's why people tend to put it off . . . and off . . . and off.

I totally get it! I'm the same when it comes to certain things: if I'm not immediately comfortable with the options in front of me, or I can't see a clear destination or outcome, I'll leave that item to sit on my to-do list for weeks, or months (or even longer!).

But here's the kicker with investing: the longer you put it off, the bigger the impact is on your ability to build meaningful wealth. On the other hand, you can magnify your chances of building wealth by proactively taking the plunge into investing.

I passionately believe everyone deserves to understand how investing works, no matter their age, gender, education level, personal history or anything else. The good news is that investing is now becoming more accessible to those who are not part of the finance industry – and women are increasingly stepping up and taking action. According to a recent ASX study, women made up 45 per cent of all new investors in Australia in 2020, up from 31 per cent among those who started five to ten years ago.[1] What's more, they're getting ahead, with female investors outperforming their male counterparts by almost 2 per cent. Meanwhile, international research from Fidelity found that 67 per cent of women are now investing outside of retirement, compared to 44 per cent in 2018.[2]

With young women engaging with the opportunities, and investing in bigger numbers than ever before, I'm thrilled to share this book with you and help give you a roadmap to guide you forward.

There's been an aura of exclusivity around investing in the past, and I think that's partly why so many of us are intimidated by the idea of it. As well, it's often made to seem more complicated than it really is. So I'm here to lift the lid on all that, and help investing make sense to you.

We're going to cover plenty in this book, including:

- Why investing *is* exciting (it's something you don't want to miss out on for the sake of Future You)!
- How money mindsets and an understanding of risk form the foundation of how we invest – psychology is really important in all this. (Having started my career in psychology I feel passionate about this point!)
- Preparing your finances so you're ready to begin your investment journey.
- An explanation of all the major asset classes (if you don't know what they are, you soon will!), followed by a deeper dive into shares and property.
- The all-important ethical side of investing.
- The role of super in your investment portfolio.
- The nitty-gritty of the numbers to prepare you for dipping a toe into investing directly in particular companies.
- An exploration of tax – why it's sexier than you think, and why it's a good idea to factor it into your investment plan.
- The major investment strategies and how you can bring everything you've learned together to create your own plan to build your future wealth.

Over the past few years, I've had the privilege of witnessing my clients and members of the She's on the Money community make huge strides on their investment journeys and I love to see the joy, satisfaction, sense of accomplishment and pride they feel as they create portfolios that reflect their lifestyles and values; and to see their wealth beginning to grow. I sincerely want you to experience the fantastic opportunities that good investments can give all of us, and to see how learning about making informed decisions on your money can be really exhilarating.

While I'm not lucky enough to work with each of you directly (if only there were more hours in the day!), I'd love for you to feel that you've got me walking next to you, looking out for you. And whether you're right at the start of your investing journey or a few steps down the track but keen to take your understanding up a level, this book is for you.

One quick caveat, friends: please keep in mind that nothing in this book should be construed as personal advice. As much as it would be dreamy for me to give you a one-size-fits-all solution, the reality is that every one of you beautiful people reading this right now has different goals, budgets, income levels, risk profiles and more. So the advice in these pages is only general. It's great to bring a financial adviser on board if you can, to tailor a plan to you personally, but I also recognise that is a privilege not available to everyone.

Okay, what are you waiting for? Let's get started!

Chapter 1

Why do people invest, anyway?

And why do I believe you can't afford NOT to invest?

Growing up, I had a better start than most when it came to financial literacy. My dad was a successful accountant so he was great with money, and he was determined to teach us everything he knew. He would say things like, 'make sure you always spend less than you earn' or 'make sure you pay yourself first' – meaning putting 5 or 10 per cent of our money away and pretending it wasn't there.

So with this great financial foundation, I was an amazing money manager from the outset, right?

Wrong. I had zero interest in learning what Dad was trying to teach me. It all seemed boring, and I often tuned out when he started talking about money.

So I never 'paid myself first'. In fact, I went through a phase of doing exactly the opposite – spending *a lot* more than I earned.

By the time I was in my early twenties, I'd racked up quite a bit of personal debt, signing my life away on credit cards and personal loans for things that had seemed so worth it at the time. I had a serious case of FOMO, and the idea of saving up to pay for everything I wanted to buy or do seemed completely impossible (and, to be honest, a bit boring). I think this is how most people feel in their twenties – invincible, impatient . . . and not thinking for a moment about how all of this spending and splurging now would impact on their capacity to reach their goals in the future.

I wanted to study overseas, so I took out a loan.

I wanted a car, so I got another loan.

Eventually, I was forking out hundreds of dollars every month in personal debt repayments. In fact, I can tell you the exact amount of money I spent on my debt each month.

It was $853. Every. Single. Month.

My wage at the time was around $50,000 a year. So handing over $853, on top of rent and bills and day-to-day living expenses, left me with no money to save or invest, and often left me feeling stressed about how I would achieve my goals.

There were times I felt like I'd never be able to get ahead. But I did. Slowly but surely, I changed my mindset and habits through learning and by understanding what my money was being spent on and where I could save. When I'd finally scrimped and saved enough to pay off all my debt and start saving, which I detail in my first book, *She's on the Money*, I started to learn about investing. And that's when things really got interesting.

My first attempt at investing

My first experience with the finance industry – outside of my dad – was meeting with a financial adviser to discuss my options for investing my savings.

I was working in organisational psychology and I'd started to become interested in the impact that investing can have. For so many of my clients, I could see that money, or lack thereof, created stress and anxiety in their lives. I'd become really passionate about the idea of investing and creating future wealth for myself, but I didn't know where to start.

I'd done plenty of research, but although I thought I was pretty smart, I knew I'd need some help. So I found a financial adviser online and made an appointment.

I was so excited on the day of the meeting. The adviser seemed so professional. He even had a whiteboard! He gave me what sounded like the standard spiel he reeled off to all prospective clients, then started asking me about my financial position. How much money did I have to invest? How much had I saved? What were my goals?

I explained to the adviser that I'd paid out all my debts and managed to save a small amount of money, something that had seemed completely unachievable to me just a couple of years earlier.

I told him I'd been learning about investing and wanted to use my savings to grow my wealth for the future.

I had $5,000 to get started, I told him.

'I can't help you,' he said, shaking his head. 'With $5,000, that's not enough to bother getting started with professional advice.'

I'll never forget the feeling that washed over me as I sat there, crushed by his response.

But I've got myself out of loads of personal debt, I thought. *Not only that, I've got myself to a point where I have savings – a consistent savings plan, which I add to every pay day. I've given up my bad habits. I've cemented positive new ones that are helping me move forward. Why won't this guy take me seriously?*

I was full of energy and enthusiasm, and I felt like he should have been congratulating me on all that I'd achieved so far and encouraging me to go out and grab all the opportunities I could find with both hands. But instead of being met by a similar vibe, I was pretty much stonewalled.

All I wanted was for someone to support my new-found enthusiasm for finance and investing, but he really didn't want a bar of me. He pretty much laid it bare. 'An investment portfolio is out of your league.'

I was *gutted*. I felt like I had wasted his time. Like he was disappointed in me for even bothering to turn up to this meeting with a paltry $5,000 to my name.

I could have let this setback stop me dead in my tracks. I could have given up and blown my $5,000 on an amazing holiday or designer handbag.

But I wasn't about to let this dude with his whiteboard and huge ego tell me what I could or couldn't achieve! Instead, I decided to educate myself further. I invested that $5,000 all by myself. I studied and gave up my job in organisational psychology to become a financial adviser. And I made it my mission to create a space where other women could get the help they needed to manage their money, without ever being made to feel stupid or small, like I had been.

Sharing the (financial) love

It didn't take long before I found my new-found passion creeping into conversations with friends. We'd go out to breakfast once a week and, after the usual chatter about boyfriends and workplace dramas, the conversation would turn to finance. I would ask how things were going money-wise and try to find subtle ways to give them a little advice, without coming across as a know-it-all.

I actually couldn't believe how well it worked! My friends were picking up on all the knowledge I was throwing out there, transforming their attitudes to money in the process. It was so exciting to see! So I thought: how can I reach and help more women, outside my circle of friends? That's when I started the She's on the Money Facebook group.

I founded She's on the Money to give other women access to empowerment, education and encouragement – all the things

I'd been chasing for such a long time. It's a community of cheerleaders, celebrating people's successes, no matter how small, and meeting their energy, wherever they are at. It's a community that I adore and am so proud to be a part of.

From the Facebook group, the podcast was born. It was supposed to be 12 episodes – a chance to speak to my community and teach them the basics – but we kept coming up with more topics. The feedback was fantastic, so I kept going. It's now snowballed into 300 episodes and counting! We have 1.2 million listeners and produce three episodes a week.

Why focus on women?

As an adviser, I've worked with women in all stages of their lives with varying levels of financial literacy.

Some don't know how many bank accounts they've got. Others don't even know what bank their accounts are with! They've often got next to no super after taking time off work to look after the kids, and they don't understand the terms of their home loan or how much they need to budget for each week or month. And that's fine, because we all have to start somewhere.

But when you consider that women over 50 are the fastest-growing demographic in terms of homelessness in this country, you can see why I'm so passionate about educating women about financial literacy. When we leave the financial management up to someone else, we give up our autonomy and control. As a financial adviser, but more importantly as a woman, this absolutely terrifies me. To think that, after a lifetime of caring for others and trusting your partner, you could end up couch surfing or sleeping in your car with nothing but a bag of clothes to your name? It's not just scary: it's unacceptable.

One of the reasons I'm so passionate about teaching women how to invest is that it's an avenue they can use to help narrow the gender gap when it comes to their retirement savings. According to a study conducted in 2018 by Monash University and Australian Super, men in Australia retire with 42 per cent more super than women.[3]

Let that sink in for a minute.

Forty-two per cent more.

That's a seriously significant difference!

And when you consider that the Association of Superannuation Funds of Australia (ASFA) calculates that a single person will need $46,494 a year to live comfortably throughout their retirement, it's easy to understand why super often isn't adequate. But the good news is that by investing throughout your working life, you can create additional wealth, allowing you to have a secure and prosperous retirement.[4]

There are a number of factors that impact on women's ability to accumulate adequate superannuation. Women are often employed in lower-paid occupations, such as childcare. As super is paid by employers as a percentage of income, lower-paid workers accumulate less super throughout their career.

Women may spend years out of the workforce entirely, caring for children or relatives, keeping in mind that paid parental leave from the government currently doesn't include super. Unpaid work in the family unit, a burden often taken on by women, doesn't come with super payments either. And when these women return to work, many do so part-time, juggling other responsibilities, which further contributes to a lower super balance when they retire.

Even women who hold down full-time roles their entire working life are at a disadvantage. Australian women in full-time roles earn around 16 per cent less than men. That's 16 per cent less super going into their fund each year. While you might think that 16 per cent is not that impactful, the knock-on effects are actually significant. Amplified over an entire lifetime, the gender pay gap greatly contributes to women being at a disadvantage no matter how hard they work.

A report by the Workplace Gender Equality Agency revealed that, along with fragmented work histories, lower-paid roles and unpaid care responsibilities, a lack of financial literacy is also contributing to women's economic insecurity in retirement.[5]

And the intimidating, hyper-masculine culture of the finance industry doesn't help one bit.

Is women in finance just another fad?

Cute question! Look, I'm going to let you in on a little secret about the finance industry – it's got to be one of the most inaccessible, ego-driven industries out there. For a start, it's hugely male-dominated. Even in places like Sweden, which is considered to be one of the most gender-equal countries in the world, industries such as investment banking have dismally low numbers of female staff. One study found that investment banking teams in Sweden had just 5 to 20 per cent female employees, with the masculine culture and long working hours cited as reasons that women are underrepresented.[6]

Even as a professional within the industry, with the credentials to back me up, I still experience it on the daily at conferences or when networking online. People are consistently surprised to learn that not only am I a successful financial adviser, but I even have my own practice. I've had people look at me in shock when they realise that I actually do know what I'm talking about! I'm constantly having to re-establish my expertise and prove myself in this industry simply because I'm a woman – and that has to stop.

That's not to say women are not represented at all. We're here, and we're growing in numbers (#represent). And yes, sometimes, some companies or governments are genuinely trying to make life better for those in marginalised groups, but surely I can't be the only one who feels like so much of it is disingenuous and tokenistic. It's become kind of trendy in the finance industry to have women on your team or your board. It makes you look good. It makes you seem ethical and progressive.

The truth remains that it's *not* a level playing field. Women still haven't achieved an equal dynamic in finance. We're not offered the same positions, opportunities or salaries as men.

It feels like a false welcome into this exclusive club. 'Oh yes, we're diverse, we employ women. But we're still going to pay you less than the man who was doing the job before you ...' Thanks – but actually no thanks!

It's a bit like when your parents had their friends over for dinner, and you'd feel so special and lucky to be given a seat at the grown-ups' table. Nobody was really listening to you or paying attention to anything you had to say. Your opinion wasn't interesting or exciting to them. But they'd done the right thing, hey? They hadn't sent you to bed early or plonked you in front of the TV. You were included ... except you weren't.

A lot of these finance industry bros would love to have you believe that they've got some kind of exclusive, insider knowledge that your lady brain couldn't possibly understand. That you need to pay big bucks for their help to even get started managing your own wealth.

In reality, with a little education and a supportive community of like-minded women behind you, you can do it on your own. You don't need a degree or an expensive financial adviser to understand the basic concepts and make decisions about investing. And you've already taken the first step by buying and reading this book!

Even if you haven't had a great upbringing when it comes to financial literacy, even if your parents never talked to you about money and you've never had to deal with finance in your day-to-day life, I promise that you can learn what you need to know to get started.

I want you to trust yourself and back yourself completely. Soak up the teachings in this book and then put them into practice.

Because you *are* smart enough. You *are* confident enough. You *can* do it. And I'm going to help you.

I'm going to help you because we need to take action. We can't afford to stand on the sidelines any longer, opting out of investing, putting it in the too hard basket or leaving it up to the other half to sort out. The gender gap is very real, no matter what grey-haired men in suits would have you believe, and as women, it's so important that we're aware of it and understand how it impacts our lives.

It's not sustainable to keep your head in the sand with this stuff – your future health and wealth literally depend on it.

Apart from the oppressive forces of the patriarchy, which have been trying to keep anyone who's not a white male in their place since the dawn of time, there are some other reasons women tend to lag behind men when it comes to investing. The good news is that these are things we can work on without dismantling our entire social system.

For a start, women are generally more cautious when it comes to taking risks and making big decisions. We take our time to consider our options and we do more research. This is *great* when it comes to investing, because it means we're less likely to jump into something silly without the proper information.

But it can also mean that we get ourselves stuck in analysis paralysis, where we spend so much time thinking and worrying about things that we don't have any time left to actually do them. Sound familiar? I know I've been there!

Another big factor is FOMO. Former US President Theodore Roosevelt is famously quoted as saying, 'Comparison is the thief of joy.'

Yet, we all do it. All the time.

I can't tell you how many times I've heard friends, clients, relatives or members of the She's on the Money community say things like:

'I have to have a house by the time I'm 30.'

'If I'm not married before 35, I'm a total failure.'

'All my friends were making six figures by the time they were 28. I feel like such a loser.'

'I can't believe I'm XX years old and I don't have the car / the job / the career / the apartment / the awards / the partner / the kids . . .'

The list goes on.

This comparison needs to stop. Seriously, I mean it. Stop right now! Stop looking at other people's goals or achievements and assuming that you need to do the same thing to be worthy or enough. It's simply not true, my friend!

Don't waste your energy or attention worrying about what other people are doing. How much they're earning. What fancy stuff they're buying. You don't even know how they're buying it! They could have a six-figure credit card debt to show for all those shiny, new 'things'.

Don't forget, everyone has their own drama going on behind closed doors. For all you know, those amazing shoes your friend just bought cost her a small fortune in interest payments each month. And that dream home? Maybe it's not such a dream inside and her marriage is falling apart. Or maybe she's really happy, living in wedded bliss. Maybe she's really good at managing money. It doesn't matter because it doesn't change *your* situation.

You're running your own race, to your own destination, and that's the only one that matters. Every time you put one foot in front of the other, every small change you make, is a positive step in the right direction.

Don't go around wishing you could be more like someone else or coveting what they have. Instead, focus on what *you* want to achieve and put the tools in place to make it happen. This is exactly what we'll be working on together in this book, and I can't wait!

'But I'm not good enough'

I'm going to take a wild leap here and assume this is something you've said to yourself more than once over the years – am I right?

We've all been the victims of Imposter Syndrome. Me included.

So, tell me, when you say you're not good enough, what do you really mean?

Good enough ... compared to what? Compared to whom? What's this unofficial, invisible standard you've pegged yourself against to arrive at the conclusion that you've fallen short?

And what is it about other people that makes you believe they *are* good enough? When you look at someone you admire, someone who seems like they've got it all figured out ... what does that look like?

Well, here's another secret for you: nobody – and I mean *nobody* – has it all figured out. It's true!

Some of us are happy in our relationships, but drowning in debt. Others have a fantastic career, but are struggling to get pregnant. Others have loads of money stashed away in savings and investments, but we're missing that special someone to enjoy it all with.

You know the perfectly polished career woman you see at the coffee shop every day, wearing designer clothes and carrying a new handbag every week? She could be secretly planning to freeze her eggs because she feels like she's never going to meet the right partner after a string of failed relationships.

Or the mum who lives in a beautiful home with a white picket fence, but hasn't had time to shave her legs in six months. She's managing to keep a couple of tiny humans and a household together, but feels disheartened every time she walks past the mirror.

Or how about the academic who has a PhD and commands huge respect from her peers, but is still living in her parents' spare room because she can't afford rent and HECS repayments on her salary?

So many achievements. So many successes. But that one mountain they just can't seem to conquer is bringing them down.

'But Victoria, you're a financial adviser. Why are you talking about relationships, kids and all this other life stuff?'

Because, at the end of the day, money is just one piece of the puzzle. Having money isn't the end goal; it's what money allows and creates and invites in that's important.

It helps us have a more comfortable, enjoyable life. When you have enough money, it reduces stress. It gives us more freedom and affords us more choices.

Ultimately, it puts us in the driver's seat.

In this book, I'm going to show you how to get from where you are now into that driver's seat. I'm going to help you set goals, understand your finances and make a plan to invest that sets you up to grow your wealth. Sound good? I thought so!

It's important to work backwards, which starts by knowing your values and pinpointing your goals. Once you know your *why*, the *how* becomes so much easier. If you have clear goals, it makes it much easier to figure out what you need to do, money-wise, to achieve them.

• •

WORKING OUT YOUR WHY

Ask yourself questions like:

- What would really make you happy, now and in the future?
- What is your ultimate target income?
- How much money in savings would feel 'safe' to you?
- What would you have to achieve to feel accomplished and successful?

- What would ultimately make you feel 'rich'?
- Are you motivated by how others perceive your goals, or do you feel most successful when a goal is personally rewarding?

Asking these types of questions allows you to get an understanding of what you're really hoping to build, grow and achieve with your money.

Once you know that end goal, your next question is this: how can you break that down into smaller, manageable chunks that you can tick off each day, week or year, to keep you motivated?

● ●

So, what's next?

I don't know about you, but I'm pumped to get going! In the chapters ahead, I'm going to help you get really clear on your financial situation: where you stand now, what your overall living costs are and what your investing options could be. Compiling a balance sheet can be pretty confronting, especially if you realise you're not in as good a financial position as you thought, but information is power. The more you know, the more decisive and action-oriented you can be – and that's what we want.

Also, you can't build a solid house on shoddy foundations. You need to get these basics right before you can tackle the more complex side of money and investments. Once you know exactly where you stand, you can move forward with confidence!

Remember, the starting point and end goal will be different for everyone. Our goals are unique, and no goal is more worthwhile or important than another. It comes down to your personal values, motivations and goals.

Some will be starting with a little (or a lot) of cash and savings stashed away. Others will discover their net worth is effectively zero once they deduct their liabilities from their assets. Others will be beginning their journey in debt – and that's okay. The important thing is to get to grips with where you're at. Then, we can start. Every step you take is a step towards financial security and prosperity.

That's the purpose of this book. It isn't to lecture or judge, or make you question or feel bad about all the decisions you've made in the past. It's to empower you to set big goals, make informed decisions and work towards your best money life!

This is an accessible, actionable guide to investing, and I hope by the time you turn the last page you'll feel confident enough to take charge of your money, grow your wealth and secure your future financial security.

● ● ● ● ● ●

TAKE NOTE

You can start preparing to invest right now,
no matter your current position.

....

You don't need to spend a lot of money on a financial adviser or study for years to get the skills. You can teach yourself the basics.

....

Every small step you take today is putting you
on the path to financial security – it's never too
early, or too late, to take that first step.

....

Chapter 2

Money mindset

We're kicking off here because it's *so* important to understand your money mindset when it comes to getting yourself set up for managing your finances, investing, and building wealth. If you've read my last book or you're familiar with the podcast (hey there!), the concept of money stories might be familiar, but it's always worth revisiting, especially if you've had a hard time previously with making positive changes.

'But Victoria, can't we just skip this part and get into the nitty-gritty of investing?'

I get it, and I'm stoked you're keen to get started. But – and this is a really big but! – if you don't understand your money mindset *before* you start, you will likely be setting yourself up to fail.

When I studied psychology, I learned all about the power of the brain – our thoughts, feelings and beliefs – to influence behaviour. It's true for pretty much any aspect of our lives, from our health to our relationships to the way we interact with money.

Getting to grips with what your money stories are and learning how to use them to your advantage is the key to success and will make you feel more fulfilled along the journey.

So before we delve into the technical investment stuff, let's explore your money mindset.

What is a money mindset?

Depending on where you fall on the spectrum of 'I'm totally here for this money mindset work' to 'Is she serious about this?!', you might be reading this and thinking, 'Victoria, I don't even *have* a money mindset. I honestly don't even think about money at all! I just know I want more of it.'

Newsflash: *that* is your money mindset! Even if you're someone who doesn't believe in the very concept of mindset in general, that in itself is a mindset.

Your money mindset is inextricably interwoven with your money story. Your money story is an entrenched belief you have, often based on your experiences growing up. You can have multiple money stories running at once. The seeds of your mindset are planted in childhood as you watch how your caregivers manage their finances. You establish your own sense of financial security (or insecurity, in many cases) based on your surroundings at home.

Determining your money mindset will help you to figure out the best way for you to approach debt and money management. Let me give you an example.

Imagine you've got three credit cards.

- Card A has a $1,000 balance at 10 per cent interest.
- Card B has a $5,000 balance at 12 per cent interest.
- Card C has a $15,000 balance at 20 per cent interest.

If you're someone who's motivated by cold, hard logic – maths and facts – you'd pay off the one with the highest interest rate first, right? You'd smash Card C with every spare dollar. It's costing you a fortune in interest and it's costing you the highest amount of interest, so you'd pay that off as quickly as possible before focusing on the other two cards.

As a financial planner, I call that **avalanching the debt**, knocking out the most expensive one first, then watching the others cascade in its wake.

But consider another option. Let's say you're someone who feels a sense of achievement in small but ongoing accomplishments. To keep yourself motivated, it might be more effective to pay down Card A first. Yes, you'll pay more interest overall, so it's not necessarily the best option from a purely financial point of view. However, it's important to factor in the psychological effect of conquering that debt. The feeling of accomplishment that comes with cutting up that first card in a matter of months, and the satisfaction of calling the bank and cancelling the account, getting rid of that debt for good. Then you can take the money you were using to pay it off and channel it into repayments on your other cards.

This method is called **snowballing**, because you gather up steam and make a bigger impact as you roll along, similar to the way a snowball grows as it rolls down a hill.

Neither method is *right* or *wrong*. One means you pay less interest; one means you close a debt off quicker. Both are effective in their own way. The one you use depends on what works best for *you*. To figure that out, you have to know yourself, your motivations and your values.

• •

THE NINE MONEY PERSONALITIES

Over the past decade or so, there has been a real boom of money personalities, online quizzes, books, courses and websites, which makes sense because it is absolutely essential that you

have a deep understanding of your attitudes towards money
and investing, and the emotions that hide behind the decisions
you make around money. Financial psychology pioneer Kathleen
Gurney found investors fit one of nine 'money personalities'.[7]
They are:

High rollers

They are thrill seekers who enjoy financial risks. For them, money
brings instant power and recognition. They're creative, extroverted
and competitive. They prefer to risk their assets rather than be
bored by financial security.

Optimists

Money brings them peace of mind; they're more interested in
enjoying it than making it grow. They're not highly involved with
their money, taxes or investments, mainly because they find it
too stressful.

Entrepreneurs

High-income earners who enjoy the power and prestige of money.
Mostly male-dominated, they're driven by a passion for excellence
and achievement. Investing in the share market is their favoured
strategy.

Hunters

Highly educated, above average income earners, they tend to
spend and invest impulsively. Mostly female-dominated, they
attribute financial success more to luck than ability and judgement.

Perfectionists

They're so afraid of making a mistake that they often avoid
decisions altogether. They'll consider every angle and find fault
with practically any risky venture. Finding suitable investments
is difficult.

Safety players

Average earners who prefer secure investments. They lack confidence and motivation to take more calculated risks, even though they may be well educated. They feel they're doing fine financially and repeat investment strategies that seem to work.

Achievers

The second-highest income earners, usually college graduates and mostly married. They feel hard work, diligence and effort will pay off. They're proud of their accomplishments and tend to recoil at other people handling their money. Protecting their assets is their primary consideration.

Money masters

They're the number one wealth accumulators even though they don't necessarily earn the most. They rank first in the degree of desired involvement with their money and enjoy the participation. They trust the recommendations of others and act on sound advice. Success through determination is their philosophy.

Producers

They rank high in work ethic but lower in earned income due to lack of self-confidence in money management skills. They work hard, desire more and feel they have difficulty getting ahead financially. Financial investment education would help.

Take some time to reflect on these nine personalities. Which one feels most aligned to you?

● ●

How to reframe your money mindset

Now you know your money mindset, let's totally unravel it and start all over again.

Just kidding! Kind of. Changing your mindset means flipping the script to one that serves you, your values and your goals.

Think about when you decide to embark on a new health regimen. You might read books and web articles, follow relevant experts and influencers on social media and tune in when friends and family claim they've lost 5 kilos on this diet or that healthy eating plan. You might learn how to read the labels on food packets properly, maybe make some notes about some of the ingredients or additives you're trying to avoid, or memorise how much fat, protein or carbs should ideally be in each serving.

All of this education is great, but it doesn't necessarily help with your internal battle, that is your entrenched mindset around food. Perhaps you associate hearty, carb-heavy pastas with a warm hug from your nanna, or you feel that a celebration can't possibly be kicked off without a glass of bubbles.

These mindset blockers need to be addressed before you get started. Otherwise, no matter how many facts and figures you memorise, these obstacles will always hold you back.

Our money mindsets are often subconscious and entrenched. They were laid in our brains decades ago, like train trackwork, and our thoughts and habits are the trains that simply follow the set line. But I'm glad to say it is possible to change your money mindset, even the really deep-rooted core beliefs. Changing your attitude towards money requires work, but it's doable. You wouldn't expect to transform a lifetime of terrible eating habits overnight, or suddenly develop the unstoppable self-confidence to audition for a TV talent show when you'd normally get nervous talking to the postie! Your money mindset is no different.

Some people are born with a glass-half-full mindset. They go through life seeing the good in everything and hoping for the best. But even if you weren't born with this mindset, it's never too late to learn it. It's not about starting from scratch; it's about figuring out what isn't working for you, so you can live with more opportunity, abundance and choice.

You don't have to delete everything you know, think or feel about money, but you do need to reframe the parts that are holding you back.

Here's why.

Thoughts create feelings and feelings create behaviours . . . which in turn create new thoughts, and the cycle begins all over again.

Until you decide to break it. And you *can* break it. You need to reframe your thoughts and feelings if you want to change your behaviour patterns, but that involves work.

Here's a great example of how you can use language as a tool for reframing your thoughts.

Think about the word 'budget'. How does that word make you feel? A lot of people would say it makes them feel restricted, or like they're missing out. It has negative connotations because it emphasises all the things you won't be able to do – not unlike how the word 'diet' puts a spotlight on all those yummy things you're no longer allowed to eat.

But what about 'spending plan' or 'financial goals'? These terms emphasise the positive parts: the cash you actually get to spend, or the goals you're going to accomplish.

Similar to reframing a 'diet' as a 'body nourishing plan', turning your 'budget' into something more affirming can help invigorate you and keep you on track.

You need to set your focus firmly on the goals you're going to achieve rather than allowing yourself to get stuck in those old ways. It can be as simple or as complicated as you'd like to make it. The important thing is to recognise what your money mindset is, and how you can tweak it to better serve you.

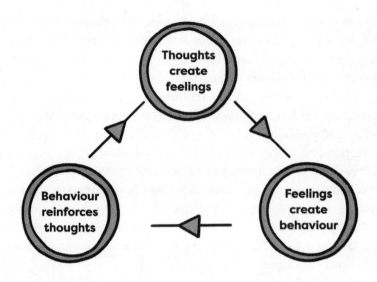

Thoughts, values, beliefs and behaviours

Research shows that our money stories start as early as seven years old,[8] when we pick up on family habits and start to internalise feelings of scarcity and abundance. I would argue that they probably begin even earlier than that, because kids are like little sponges and there's not much they don't soak up.

Those of us who grew up without much in the way of material things, who maybe had parents who struggled to put food on the table, can become super risk-averse. We might feel guilty investing or spending money on ourselves because our parents never had enough. We might be cautious about spending money on anything 'non-essential' because we're subconsciously worried we won't have enough money to get by. The irony is that this mindset actually limits us from growing our wealth.

This is a very common money mindset – and, happily, one that can be undone.

On the flipside, other people who missed out when they were younger might be determined to live it up as much as they can, now that they have a good income. They're not afraid to splash cash on designer outfits. Their kids are totally spoilt because they want them to have the childhood they themselves missed out on. They don't save for tomorrow because life is too short.

It's a completely different reaction to the situation, but the result is pretty much the same – you're short-changing yourself in the long run by letting those ghosts haunt you.

Whatever your past, you have to make peace with it and, instead of letting it hold you back, use it to help you move forward in a positive way.

This is a good time to mention that there's no such thing as a 'good' or 'bad' money story – there are just stories. They lead to a range of different outcomes, and if you feel like your money story is working for you, then there's no need to make big changes. So while you can't alter the past, you *can* change how it affects your present and your future.

Tapping into your own money story and mindset is also a great way to better understand your friends and family, and their money energy.

If you have a friend who always orders the cheapest thing on the menu, or gets their iPhone out to calculate *to the cent* how much they owe when splitting the bill, you might think it's because they're super stingy or frugal with money. But when you're more aware of your own money mindset, you'll be able to understand that their paranoia or need for control around money stems from their own experiences. It could be that very real trauma has impacted their money mindset. Maybe they grew up in poverty, or fled an abusive relationship where they had no autonomy when it came to financial decisions. Maybe they grew up with good financial security, but they somehow absorbed the money message that you need to hold on to every dollar you earn.

I once knew a woman whose family was loaded – they owned five restaurants and had substantial seven-figure wealth behind them. But her parents fretted about money constantly, and she grew up thinking they were struggling to make ends meet. It wasn't until she was well into her twenties that she realised, 'Hey, my family is actually really well off!'

There's almost always a reason why people are the way they are and think the way they do. When you've studied psychology, it's pretty hard to get annoyed with anybody about anything, because you realise that most of us are products of our past circumstances. And when you tune into other people's money stories, it suddenly all starts to make sense.

It's not just about money stories, though. Our mindset and belief systems around everything in life start when we're really young, from those memories we don't even really remember, yet they're imprinted somewhere in the back of our brains and they inform how we think and feel about so many things in ways that we don't even realise most of the time.

● ●

TAKE A LOOK BACK

Examining how those formative years have helped make us who we are today can be confronting, but it can also be really empowering – and it gives you the opportunity to do something about it.

So ask yourself:

- How much has your childhood influenced the choices you've made as an adult?
- Has the dynamic between your parents impacted your relationships?
- Has their attitude towards money steered you down a particular path?

Until you know something, you can't change it. Talking to a professional or a trusted friend might help you formulate your answers, or even just sitting down for some focused reflection time to really think about it.

I have to warn you: sometimes asking these questions and going deep into this work can mean opening up a *biiig* can of worms. It might get uncomfortable. There may be a few tears shed. But I promise you, it'll be worth it, because it will put you back in the driver's seat of your life.

• •

Once you know your money mindset, how do you set realistic goals?

Setting realistic, achievable goals is central to rewriting your money story. I talk about goal-setting at length in my first book, but here's a quick reminder.

We've all heard about SMART goals, right? We know our goals should be Specific, Measurable, Achievable, Relevant, and Time-bound. Well, at She's on the Money we've got our own goal-setting framework, which is a little bit different.

Instead of SMART goals, we set SOTM goals – Specific, Optimistic, Time-bound, and Measurable. The optimistic bit is key, because it focuses on our mindset, our self-confidence and our self-belief.

Now, I personally prefer to work on a few goals at a time, but on different timescales. That might include a couple of short-term goals, like a weekend away or a new pair of shoes, along with a couple of medium-term goals, such as upgrading your car, and a long-term goal, like buying a property.

CATEGORISE YOUR GOALS

Let's take a moment to write down a bunch of your financial goals and put them into categories we can work with: short-, medium- and long-term.

Write all your goals here – even if they seem totally unachievable. That's what the 'optimistic' bit is for!

Short-term: ....

....

....

Medium-term: ....

....

....

Long-term: ....

....

....

Letting go of limiting beliefs and embracing your values

Achieving the goals you've just written down depends on believing in yourself and your abilities.

Let me ask you a question: have you ever really wanted to do something or have something – it could be studying to become a midwife, or buying your first home, or meeting the love of your life – but no matter what you do, you can't shut off that little voice in the back of your mind? You know the voice I'm talking about; the one that whispers, 'You're not smart enough, good enough, successful enough, rich enough, loveable enough to get that . . .'

Even when the logical, practical part of your brain knows that's not true, there's something very powerful about that little voice that plants seeds of doubt and shakes your confidence.

What if I told you that there are loads of people out there right now, succeeding in various areas of their lives, kicking goals in business and relationships . . . and they're not better or smarter or more talented than you? They're kicking those goals because they believe in themselves. That's the power of self-belief. Without it, most of us would struggle to do anything. With it, we can conquer everything!

Self-belief is *huge*. It is bound up with our values, because when we care about something enough, when we value it and prioritise it, we somehow manage to summon up the self-belief we need to make it happen.

When you live in harmony with your values, everything becomes easier. Aligning your money mindset with your values helps foster pride in your accomplishments. It allows you to shed all that guilt you've been carrying around with you, weighing you down, so you can save and spend confidently.

Everyone's values will be different, and there's not necessarily a right or wrong. Well, okay, there are some things that are obviously wrong – I'm not saying it's okay to go around committing crimes or hurting people because you've decided those are your values! But within the spectrum of non-criminal behaviour that doesn't infringe upon the rights of others, all values are worthy and valid.

Perhaps you really value health and wellbeing? Your body is your temple, so you see spending money on yoga classes and an organic fruit and veggie box each week as an investment in that asset. Or maybe family is your 'why', and you're happy to take a pay cut and work three days a week so you can help out at your child's kinder, or take your nanna out for lunch once a week.

Ploughing your time and energy into those relationships is worth more to you than money.

I've got a friend who treats herself to a weekly massage. Yep, every Friday she's topless, lying face down in a dark room, with relaxing music, calming essential oils, and pampering for an entire hour. Every. Single. Week!

I wouldn't spend my money on a weekly massage, but only because that doesn't align with my values. Me? I love to go out to eat. I adore decadent dinners with my girlfriends, where we dress up and splurge on good food and champagne at really great restaurants. I order meals I would never even attempt to cook at home. Once, I had the most incredible creamy, rich scalloped potato dish, where the potatoes had been sliced into pieces and twice-fried. I still salivate a little bit just thinking about it. Crispy on the outside, soft and gooey on the inside. I would've paid for them three times over, that's how good they were.

I'm happy to pay a little more for high-quality dining experiences, because that's one of my values. I truly relish every mouthful of the food, knowing I don't have the skills or the time to create it in my own kitchen. And, touching on all that mindset stuff again, there's definitely a part of me that associates delicious food with friendship, family and happiness – it enhances my relationships, and makes me feel loved.

While I'm out living it up during these monthly dinners, my friend is happy to plonk herself on the couch with microwaved leftovers from last night's home-cooked meal. I mean, she's probably *waaay* too relaxed from all those massages to bother going out for dinner anyway!

The point is, we're both doing what makes us happy – we're both living true to our values, and spending our time and money accordingly.

The thing with money (and time, as it turns out) is that you can have pretty much anything you want – but you can't have everything.

You can have an amazing luxury car – even on a pretty average income – if you're prepared to live on beans on toast and spend a huge chunk of salary on the repayments.

You can travel the world, holiday overseas every year for weeks at a time, no matter what your salary – but you might have to come back to a tiny one-bedroom flat full of hand-me-down furniture, if that's all your budget will allow.

You can work your butt off for a huge wage at the expense of your social life, or prioritise your downtime in exchange for a lower bank balance.

These are sacrifices and choices we make every day. When you know your values, you empower yourself to make the decisions that make you happiest.

More fancy dinners, fewer massages.

More me-time and lower car repayments.

More expensive hobbies, but smaller apartment.

More of the family budget on private school fees for the kids, but fewer overseas holidays.

It's all about prioritising what aligns with your values.

So, here's the fun part: what are your values?

Be honest with yourself – the only one you're answering to here is you. So don't say what you think is the 'right' thing to say. Don't worry about how anyone else would respond to the same question. Just think about what really matters to you, deep down.

What could you give up in a heartbeat if you had to?

What would you cling on to for dear life, and sacrifice other stuff in order to achieve?

If you need help figuring out your values, you can turn back to the section on this topic in *She's on the Money*.

● ● ● ● ● ●

VERONICA, 28 – VIC

I always worry that there isn't enough money. Growing up, I had a comfortable childhood up until I was 12. Then when my mum passed away, my dad got really depressed and we struggled with money. My dad also passed away when I was 21, and seeing the struggles with money we went through over those nine years still haunts me. Now I earn good money and save a lot of it, but I still beat myself up for not saving enough, as I'm always worried that something will happen and I will need more.

BREANNA, 28 – VIC

I have a lot of limiting beliefs and most of these are around not talking about money or only seeing the bad. I knew my parents had credit cards and I wasn't really taught to save for anything specific, just that saving was good. But because I never had something to work towards, it always faltered. We never spoke about money much at home and I feel like I'm at odds a lot when I compare where I thought I would be and where I am now. Looking back, I can see where I just sat back and 'played safe' or didn't change something out of laziness or lack of understanding and I can see where those decisions are still impacting me now.

CODY, 24 – SA

I have always been taught to save my money and I have always been good at it, however, now I feel awful whenever I spend it – even on necessary purchases or luxuries I have saved for. I became disabled when I was sixteen and it restricted a lot of employment opportunities for me. This makes me deeply concerned about my financial future and does not help my anxiety around spending money. I am from a privileged background and probably don't need to stress as much as I do, but I do want to live independently at some stage.

● ● ● ● ● ●

TAKE NOTE

Changing your money mindset is a very
personal journey and will take work.

....

You can only achieve your goals if you believe
in yourself and your abilities.

....

Everyone will have different goals, so prioritise your own happiness
and values when deciding on your short- and long-term goals.

....

Chapter 3

Understanding the big R: Risk

I can tell you're tempted to skip this chapter. Honestly, I was tempted to skip writing it! Who wants to sit down and write a few thousand words about risk?! Or even *think* about it?!

But here's the thing. Financial literacy is something I talk about a lot, and risk is a huge part of this process. It would be negligent of me to write this book without at least dipping our toes into the risk discussion. I promise I will make learning about risk as interesting as it is important!

Consider this.

You've been saving to buy a brand-new car for two years. You've been dreaming about it. When you're on the bus to work, you see this particular car everywhere. You have always wanted a cherry-red car and finally – *finally* – you're driving it out of the parking lot, feeling like a million bucks as you journey home in your stylish new ride.

Then, 300 metres from your home, you get rear-ended. Your brand-new, precious, sparkling car is suddenly smashed to pieces (well, her behind is, at least).

When you left the car park, did you take the risk of driving out of there without insurance? Or did you think to yourself, 'Hell no, there's no way I'm leaving without protecting my incredible new car.' Either way, you made an assessment of risk based on the situation and your own personal risk appetite, which then prompted you to make a decision.

We make choices like this every single day. Understanding risk is a form of financial literacy, which is in turn a form of personal insurance. It's your way of protecting yourself from future disaster, so you can feel confident that the choices you make now won't have dire consequences down the track.

The truth about risk

Unless you're a base-jumping, deep-sea-diving daredevil, you probably bristle a bit when you hear the word 'risk'. I get it.

Like a lot of the language around money and finance, 'risk' is a loaded term that carries negative connotations for many people. We spend most of our lives trying to avoid risks. We wear seatbelts, look both ways when we cross the road, make sure our medical and dental check-ups are up-to-date. We spend a lot of time, money and energy keeping ourselves safe.

I'm not necessarily recommending that you take risks every day, but I do want you to understand them. The truth is, doing nothing at all with your finances is a risk. If you choose to put your head in the sand and keep it there, you run the risk of never getting ahead – or worse, you'll end up going backwards.

It's really important to understand that the absence of making a choice is still a choice.

'But Victoria, hold on a minute! If I don't take risks I'll just stay right where I am. I'll stay safe. Sure, I won't get any huge rewards, but going backwards? That's a bit dramatic, don't you think?'

No, I don't think.

Thanks to things like inflation and rising property prices, if you keep your money under the bed (or, the modern-day equivalent, in an everyday savings account, earning pitiful interest), then increases in the cost of living over time will mean that your cash is worth less in a few years' time than it is today.

Even literally keeping your money in an envelope under your mattress carries risk. What if your home burns down? Or you're robbed? (Side note: Please, *please* don't leave large sums of cash lying around your home!)

The other thing about the perception of risk is that it's quite often totally irrational.

For example, I know plenty of people who are terrified to invest in shares (outside of their super) because they think the risk of losing money is so high, but are more than happy to invest in real estate. In fact, they think having an investment property is a fantastic idea! This is partly because property is tangible. You can see it, touch it, insure it. We're all familiar with houses, because we live in them. If you have already bought a home of your own, then you're familiar with the process of attending inspections, getting finance, submitting offers and exchanging contracts.

So, for many, property feels like a safe investment.

Now, I'm not saying it's not a good option. But is it always the best option? And is it the best option for you?

Is it really 'less risky' to borrow hundreds of thousands of dollars, invest in a huge asset, be responsible for keeping another person or persons safe and trust them to look after your property, all with a goal that your property asset will go up in value . . . is that inherently less risky than doing some research and using your savings to invest in shares of a quality company?

Some property types, in some cities, have grown in value a phenomenal amount. But a couple of things to remember here.

Property is not a liquid asset. You can't chop off a spare bedroom and trade it in for some cash if you have a medical emergency and need $10,000, stat. Your wealth is tied up in those four walls until you sell. And selling is a pain, even in a booming market. You have to fix broken things, repaint, make the garden look respectable. You'll need to find an agent to sell it, pay for photos and marketing, and get it ready for people to traipse through when it's open for inspection. Selling a property, even an investment that you don't live in, takes a lot of time, money and effort. Again, I'm not saying that property isn't a good investment, but just like all kinds of investments, it comes with risks and drawbacks that are important to understand before you invest.

There's also been many people jumping on the cryptocurrency bandwagon over the last few years. The same people who are too scared to buy shares in Australian and international companies, which are 100 years old and have proved their ability to withstand wars, economic crises and cultural shifts, seem to be okay with the risk of throwing their cash at a brand-new asset class that the vast majority of people don't even understand. Go figure!

The media has a lot to answer for here. They love to run stories about the dude who was a struggling blue-collar worker, but was lucky enough to buy low and sell high before everyone else cottoned on to whatever cryptocurrency he's into, and now he lives on a yacht and makes a hundred grand a minute, even when he's sleeping.

I don't know if this guy on the news is genuine, or how much money he's *actually* making while he snores in his Egyptian cotton sheets, but I'm gonna go out on a limb and say that whatever success he might have had, it probably can't be replicated. Whatever he's selling, I'm not buying it.

Another ironic perception I'd like to point out is that people are very quick to trust social media influencers. For every certified financial planner, budgeting expert or genuine investment guru on Instagram, there are hundreds of influencers with no knowledge or experience whatsoever, hoping to persuade you to sign up to their crypto scheme, buy their course that will teach you how to trade NFTs or make $200,000 in a week on the share market.

Would you let your dentist service your car? Would you trust the neighbour's kid who mows your lawn to fix your teeth? Then why on earth would you think it's a good idea to take investment advice from social media influencers?

I really can't emphasise it enough because I care about your financial future: don't take important (and potentially life-changing) advice from people who don't have the runs on the board.

A small amount of success over the short term does not make them an expert.

A large following on social media does not mean they know what they're doing.

And always remember those wise words: if it sounds too good to be true, it probably is! Fortunately for consumers, the Australian Securities and Investments Commission (ASIC) now requires 'finfluencers' to adhere to the same financial services laws as all professional financial advisers.

Another thing to remember about blogs, social posts and paid partnerships is that any advice they offer is very broad in nature (She's on the Money's included!). It's not attuned to your specific circumstances, your goals or your risk profile. It's illegal to give personal advice in a broad format like that, so everything communicated in these formats is general.

Which is a great place to start. It's a really good way to work out which types of investments interest you and which ones you want to learn more about. But before you part with your hard-earned money, you need to take the time to understand not only your specific risk profile, but your goals and your ethics too. These all help you decide on an investment strategy that works for you. We're talking couture, friends, not off-the-rack!

Your individual risk tolerance

A huge part of my role as a financial adviser is to assess clients' risk tolerance and then tailor my advice to match.

No two people have an identical risk tolerance because none of us are exactly the same. While some of us live in permanent YOLO-mode, others keep a first-aid kit, spare set of underwear and a muesli bar in every single handbag we own, 'just in case'. The rest of us exist somewhere in between, with our own set of personal quirks.

That's why no two Statements of Advice (which is the outline and recommendations that financial planners create for you) look the same – because when we factor in your unique risk tolerance, your ethics, values and lifestyle, and how far away from retirement you are, the best course of action will be individual to you.

Now, if you're reading this book and you're under 35, the good news is that you don't necessarily need to take on as much risk as someone older, because you've got more time on your side.

Even if you are a little older, that doesn't mean you should sink your life savings into a dodgy get-rich-quick scheme. There are safe, proven and stable ways to build wealth. It's all about how to access them and make investment decisions you feel comfortable with.

Opposites attract?

What if you're in a couple and you have wildly different attitudes to risk? Maybe your other half would happily risk it all in online poker, and you're more of an everything-in-savings kinda gal?

This is actually way more common than you might think. I've often counselled couples to appreciate and work together towards common goals despite their different risk tolerances. In these situations, communication is key.

You need to understand where the other person is coming from – remember how we talked about money stories, and how our upbringing can have a major influence on our attitude to finance? Maybe your partner's money story is very different from your own. You can't change that, but you can do your best to make sure your goals and values are aligned moving forward. You'll need to balance the information that's available to you and thoroughly research your options.

I've heard people say things like, 'But Brad at work said crypto is the way to go,' or they're reading the *Financial Review* and trying to teach themselves the ins and outs of the ASX. Meanwhile, their partner has come from a family of tradies and has been brought up to believe that property is the ideal way to invest.

This is where it pays to remember that not all sources of information are equal (that's why you weren't allowed to reference Wikipedia in your uni essays!), so we need to filter out that non-expert info and focus on the good stuff.

When your goals and values are in sync, getting the risk bit lined up becomes a little easier. So, it's important you're tracking towards the same destination as your partner before you try to figure out how much risk you're both comfortable with.

In my first book, I created an activity called 'What type of investor are you?' If you haven't done this activity before (or if you need a refresher!), this is a really simple way to assess your risk tolerance and work out which type of investment could be the right fit for you. You'll find it in Chapter 13 of this book, too, because I'm generous like that!

● ●

WHAT ABOUT SUPERANNUATION?

What's your super invested in? Are you in a balanced fund? Do your investments lean more towards the risky end of the spectrum? Most people don't even know there are options!

This is another area where your attitude towards risk is really important. It can seriously impact your financial results, but most people don't even give it a second thought.

Take a minute to go and find your most recent superannuation statement – go on, do it now, I'll wait.

Got it? Okay, great.

Now have a look at what you're invested in and how much you're paying in fees and insurance. What do you think, at first glance? Is your super really working for you?

You don't need to be a financial adviser or a maths whizz to interpret it. Just look at the cold, hard facts on that statement and ask yourself: are you happy with its level of growth? Are you happy with how much you're paying in fees? What could that mean for your future?

Furthermore, when I said to go grab your most recent statement, did you grab three or four statements, because your super is dotted all over the place in different funds?

A lot of people, especially young people, don't care about super, and that frustrates the hell out of me! Your super is, quite literally, 10.5 per cent of *everything* you earn as an employed human being. It's being invested on your behalf for your future, and it's in a tax-friendly environment. Super has the lowest taxation rate possible in Australia, meaning you are basically getting a benefit just by using the superannuation system, yet so many people don't take advantage of it!

Let me say again, just in case my message isn't quite clear enough: your super is *super* important. You might think that, because you're young, you don't need to worry about it, but that's where you're wrong. If you're young, that means you have time up your sleeve to make the most of your super. It's the *perfect* time to do something proactive about it! Trust me, Future You will be so grateful.

And if you're edging closer to your forties and above, it's just as important for you to pay attention to your super. The decisions you make today will impact the wealth you have in the future, so this is not a conversation you can afford to dip out of.

Of course, an adviser can help you with this, but here are a few things to consider:

How much risk are you willing to take? You may find you have your super in a higher risk profile, but switching to a conservative profile may be better for you if you're older.

Do you have multiple funds? If you have more than one fund, you might be paying more than one set of fees.

Are your investments aligned to your ethics? You might be surprised to discover your super fund invests in tobacco farms, fossil fuels or other industries that don't align with your values.

Here's what $10,000 would look like if you invested it in super as extra voluntary contributions versus taking it home as pay with the relevant marginal tax rate applied:

Marginal tax rate 2021–22	Net value of $10,000 take-home pay	Net value of $10,000 put into super	Difference in dollars	Difference in percentages
$45,001–$120,000				
$5,092 plus 32.5c for each $1 over $45,000	$6,750	$8,500	$1,750	21%
$120,001–$180,000				
$29,467 plus 37c for each $1 over $120,000	$6,300	$8,500	$2,200	26%

$180,001 and over				
$51,667 plus 45c for each $1 over $180,000	$5,500	$8,500	$3,00	35%

Tax year 2022–23

(Note: if your income and concessional contributions total more than $250,000 in 2022–23, you may have to pay an additional 15 per cent tax on some or all of your super contributions.)

No investment vehicle enables you to get those instant returns like super does. Yet most of us put thinking about it on the backburner until we're nearing retirement age. So we'll return to it in Chapter 9.

● ●

WHAT ABOUT SELF-MANAGED SUPER FUNDS?

A self-managed superannuation fund (SMSF) is attractive to a lot of people because it gives them the comfort of control. Now, I'm not saying you cannot start a SMSF, but what I will say is that they are hugely misunderstood and romanticised, so think really carefully before you go down that path.

SMSFs are a lot more work and responsibility than most people realise. There is tons of paperwork and documents to sign, and while you don't pay 'fees' as such, you do need to pay for auditing and accounting. Depending on your super balance, a SMSF may not be a cost-effective option, and could end up causing you a lot more stress than is necessary.

Personally, I'm not a fan of SMSFs unless there's a really bloody good reason for having one. If you've been advised to have a SMSF because of your unique circumstances, sure. Maybe you want to invest your super in property, or you have complex affairs that are better channelled through a SMSF for tax reasons. But wanting to be in control? From my perspective, that's not a reason to have a SMSF.

You can have control in a managed fund. In fact, you can have control in so many different types of super funds. In Australia, superannuation is pretty flexible and one day, it will be your biggest asset. You can invest in almost any asset class you're interested in through super – shares, property, tech, cash, fixed interest . . . You can even choose a fund that aligns with your ethics and values. What was that about wanting to have control again?

● ●

Coming back to risk

It may seem like we got a little off topic there, but the truth is, it's all connected.

Your risk appetite directly influences the decisions you make.

Now, I'm not saying any one asset class is 'bad' or not worth investing in. What I'm saying is that education is key. Many people don't know enough about the investing options they're looking at in order to make an informed decision. It's important to remember that risk is personal, and that's why nobody but you can determine what you are and are not willing to accept when it comes to risk.

Crypto is a really good example of this. I know so many people who have bought crypto because it seems like a good idea and lots of people are doing it. There is an element of behavioural finance to be unpacked here, which is really about understanding what drives people to make decisions. This is known as the Behavioural Finance Curve.

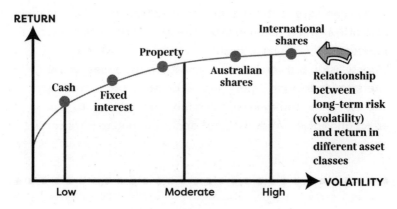

Risk–return trade-off

We covered these drivers in detail in Chapter 2, and here's how they look in practice. Essentially, the graph confirms that the higher the return, the higher the risk. Conversely, the lower the risk, the lower the return. Therefore . . .

If you stick with safe, low-key, proven investing options, you'll generally get a solid but lower return on your money.

If you're prepared to take a risk, to test the waters and see what the outcome might be even if you don't have solid proof that it's likely to be a winner, then you have the chance to earn higher rewards. But that chance comes with a higher risk.

Most common investing risks to consider

Renowned investor Warren Buffett has been famously quoted as saying 'Be fearful when others are greedy, and be greedy when others are fearful.'[9] This is basically a commentary about weighing up the risks and opportunities of the options in front of you and not necessarily following the path most commonly trodden.

Remember that by sitting on the fence or delaying taking action, you are actually making a choice. You're choosing to do nothing and, as we mentioned earlier, doing nothing has risks.

When it comes to the risks involved in investing, some of the common ones include:

Trying to time the market

I've said it before and I'll say it again: if I could time the market, I'd be a very wealthy woman! Sadly, I can't. When investing, know that there's not a 'perfect' time to get into the market – the perfect time for you is actually when you're ready, regardless of how the market is performing. So the smart thing to do is make yourself comfortable by getting fully prepared and informed *first*.

Rushing into investment because everyone else is

I'm going to use crypto as an example again here. Lots of people bought into crypto in 2021 after hearing all the hype from friends, in the media or online – despite there being no significant historical data to inform their investment choices.

Those same people are now feeling the volatility of the market, and those who invested exclusively in crypto rather than diversifying into the share market because they thought it was too 'risky', may be significantly out of pocket. At the time of writing, there is a broad sell-off amid extreme fear among investors. Bitcoin, for example, is sitting at its lowest value in the past 18 months, the media hype around its value has worn off and interest has dissipated.

Why did this happen? People were buying in part because of the strong social element. It was FOMO rather than informed, risk-assessed investing that aligned to their risk profile. It's a massive gamble to follow advice from random unqualified people – like your friend's uncle's workmate – and those who do are taking on huge amounts of risk without comprehending what they're doing.

Inflation risk

I find that plenty of people forget to factor inflation into their investing equation. I mentioned earlier in the book how the effect of inflation can mean that your purchasing power is reduced over time, so that the future real value of the asset declines. Not exactly a dream scenario, but the fact is inflation happens so we need to factor it in. The risk comes when you fail to anticipate inflation and its potential impact on your portfolio – plus there's a chance that it could be higher than predicted.

Any asset or income stream that's denominated in money tends to be more vulnerable to inflation risk (bonds in particular), whereas physical assets and equity are generally less susceptible.

'But Victoria, how do we anticipate inflation risk?'

The good news is, it's quite straightforward to build an inflation premium into your calculation of the return you hope to see, to help mitigate against its future effects. We'll come back to this later!

Currency risk

This is one for my international friends, in particular! I know there are lots of you in the She's on the Money community who come from wonderful overseas locations. If you hold investments in a foreign country, note that there's risk associated with the exchange rate between the currency in that country and the currency here. If, for some reason, there were big fluctuations in the exchange rate, that's likely to have a knock-on effect on the value of your investments in that country. You also need to be aware of currency risk if you decide to invest in assets outside of Australia, for example US shares, which are traded in US currency.

Volatility and market risk

At the end of the day, you simply can't guarantee that the value of stock or other asset will increase. The fundamental risk exists that the value could go down and cause a loss of capital, so that's something to be prepared for, both financially and psychologically.

● ● ● ● ● ●

MARI, 25 – VIC

My whole life has been pretty stable financially, but the two big stories I get stuck on are that investing is far too risky to bother with, and that the housing bubble will burst at any given moment. Through podcasts like She's on the Money *I've been able to shape my money story according to my risk appetite and I'm slowly unwinding the nerves that come with the thought of buying a first home at the wrong time. There is still a way to go and I still need to make the leap to go for that first house, but I'll get there.*

LAURA, 29 – ACT

For a long time, I just went with the super fund I got with my first job at sixteen. During COVID, I swapped jobs and I was able to join an industry-specific super fund. I did extensive research before making the switch and I was impressed with how helpful their team was. I've been able to choose an investment strategy that aligns with both my risk profile and my personal values, and I was excited to join a fund that doesn't invest in fossil fuels and has such a customer-centric focus.

● ● ● ● ● ●

TAKE NOTE

Wrapping your head around risk is an important part
of financial literacy and helps you protect yourself
from future disaster. Don't underestimate it!

....

As well as learning about your own money stories, understanding
your partner's money story and risk appetite will help you make
sure your goals and values are aligned moving forward.

....

Ideally your super will align with your risk tolerance.
Dedicating some time to getting it sorted while
you're young will do wonders for your future.

....

Chapter 4

Getting your ducks in a row

I'm going to ask you a question, and I want you to *really* think about your answer.

What's the most expensive thing you've ever bought...on credit?

Was it a handbag?

A beautiful pair of shoes?

An incredible overseas holiday?

Now, I want you to ask yourself: why did you want to buy that thing or service or experience? And who did you *really* buy it for?

Perhaps you wanted to impress someone, or fit into a certain crowd. Maybe you wanted to have that feeling, the one that implies to anyone who's interested that you've 'made it'?

I totally understand that feeling of wanting to celebrate your success and enjoy nice things. I'm no stranger to it! However, as I talked about in my last book, there's a big difference between having 'wealth' and being 'rich'. When you really break it down, rich is a type of personal style, like goth or emo or sports-luxe. Rich is the way you look when you're wearing designer everything and stepping out of a fancy car.

'Rich' is just an image.

Wealth, on the other hand, isn't something you can spot simply by looking at someone. Some of the wealthiest people I know drive old cars, mend their clothes when they start falling apart, and cook at home every single night. Unless you hacked into their internet banking (and please don't do that!), you'd never know they had wealth.

If you've been robbing your future self of life-changing wealth in order to look or feel rich now, this is my call to *stop*.

When we go into debt, we commit a portion of our future earnings to pay it off. You'll be paying, ongoing, for something you already have, or have already used, for months or years after the shiny-new appeal has worn off. And that's money we can't spend on other things that would make us genuinely happy, or save towards the future.

This is not a trade-off you want to make, right? No one wants to be temporarily rich if that puts your ability to create more permanent, lasting wealth at risk.

That's why this chapter is all about making sure we create a solid foundation on which to get started building that life-changing wealth.

Let's get to the bottom of some investing myths

In my years in the industry, I've found that people who are reluctant to invest tend to share a few common misconceptions. So before we get into what investing actually involves, let's debunk these baseless assumptions.

It's too expensive!

People think investing is expensive, but I'm here to tell you that not investing is far more expensive in the long run. Money stashed in your savings account won't even keep pace with inflation. Investing is one way to insure yourself against future rises in your cost of living.

It's too risky!

There's that 'r' word again! In many situations in life, it's the doom and gloom stories that receive the most attention. Scandals and sob stories sell. And when we hear about the failures of others, it makes it seem as though there's a high likelihood that we'll fail too. But that's simply not true.

Pay careful attention to who you listen to, and don't take everything at face value. When you get down to the nitty-gritty of why these people failed, you might find some clues. Like their shares tanked during the GFC so they panicked, sold everything and crystallised their losses. Or they went gung-ho into an investment their mate at the pub suggested, without doing any independent research.

Risk is relative. What's risky for one person may not be risky for another. It's all about what you can afford to lose.

You need to be rich!

So many people think you need to be rich already in order to make money from investing. And it's true that a lot of the mega-rich people in the world got a pretty decent hand-up from an inheritance or windfall of some kind.

However, there are also plenty of self-made millionaires out there, proving that you don't need to be rich to get started. Got $2,000? You're good to go. Does working with $2,000 seem a little ambitious? That's cool, let's look into micro-investing.

Any tiny amount you can set aside to invest can help grow your wealth.

I'd be locking my money away

Have you ever been stuck somewhere, unable to grab your phone? You know it's there, but you just can't quite reach it. Isn't it an awful feeling? We've come to depend on our smartphones so much that we feel naked and vulnerable if we don't have access to them at all times.

That's how a lot of people feel about money. They don't like the idea that their funds are locked away in an investment. It terrifies them that they might not be able to access them when required. Funnily enough, a lot of the people who say this are the same people who think buying an investment property is a fantastic idea – how ironic is that? I mean, property is one of the hardest assets to get rid of if you need cash fast, yet these people are reluctant to invest in shares . . .

The truth is, there are very few investments that genuinely 'lock' your money away. And these are often the exact kinds of investments people seem to think of as more liquid than shares. Most liquid investments allow you to access your funds within a few days, and if you need money in the meantime, that's what your emergency fund is for (more info on that later in this chapter).

I'm not an expert!

You don't have to be an expert. You just have to be committed to doing the basics of the research, so you don't make uninformed decisions.

Worried you're not 'educated' enough to know what to do or where to start? Um, hello! That's why you're reading this book! Now, I'm not pretending that by the time you've finished reading you'll be qualified to trade on Wall Street or anything, but you'll certainly be equipped with the essential knowledge you need to get started, and to know where to find additional resources if you need them.

But I could lose everything!

We've all heard the horror stories of that uncle/friend's ex/lady from your mum's Pilates class who lost every cent they had in some kind of investment-gone-bad. And these stories absolutely do exist. It is important to understand why.

Did those people invest in quality shares – like the top companies that superannuation funds invest into – and diversify their portfolio? If the bottom fell out of those kinds of shares, the very fabric of society as we know it would quite literally collapse. It'd be more of a zombie apocalypse kind of scenario than an 'Oh no! I've lost all my money and will have to move in with my nan and drink lukewarm tea forever' situation!

Losing everything is only possible if you risk everything.

● ●

WHAT ARE YOUR LONG-TERM LIFESTYLE GOALS?

When it comes to planning for the future, it looks different for everyone. To determine what your future goals mean for your investment plans, some questions to ask yourself include:

- At what age would you like to retire? Will you retire completely, or cut back to part-time for a few years first?

  ....

  ....

- What kind of income would you need to have a comfortable retirement? Think about how you plan to spend your twilight years – playing golf, travelling, dining out? Remember, your expenses will be different from what they are right now. Hopefully you'll have your home paid off, so you won't be servicing a mortgage. You may not need income protection insurance anymore, and the years of paying for gymnastics classes for the kids will be behind you.

....

....

• What legacy do you want to leave behind? It could be helping your kids buy their first homes, or contributing towards private school fees for the grandkids.

....

....

• What does retirement look like for you? A yacht in the Bahamas? A campervan travelling around Australia?

....

....

• •

Can I start investing if I'm in debt?

I can't tell you how many times I've been asked this question. I know it's a really big 'chicken or egg' question for those who want to get themselves on the right financial footing to build a better financial future.

So, is it possible?

My answer is: it's a little more complicated than a simple yes or no.

Before we start, I want to mention something about debt. It might not apply to your situation, but chances are you know someone who'll be able to relate.

Being debt-free is an enormous privilege.

That's not a popular opinion – many of you reading this will be thinking, 'Hey, Victoria! I've actually worked super-hard to pay off my debts, it's not a privilege.' Or, 'Do you have any idea of the luxuries I've gone without in order to get to my age without accumulating any debt?'

I'm not for one moment doubting your hard work, or the sacrifices that anyone has made to get out of debt.

However.

It's *still* a privilege.

For some people, getting into debt isn't a choice they've made. They haven't decided one day that a flashy car or big overseas trip is worth going into debt for. They haven't spent beyond their means and racked up reckless debts due to poor choices and bad habits.

Some people have had literally no other option than to go into debt because otherwise they would have ended up homeless or starving or without anywhere for them and their kids to sleep at night.

Single parents. People on the disability pension. Older women who've been through a marriage breakdown and have been left with no super and no savings, after decades of looking after others.

People who've used their credit card to buy their children a school uniform, or shoes that aren't falling apart. They may have ended up in debt with their electricity company because they had to use that money to pay their car registration so they could get to work. Or they fell behind in their rent because they had a huge, unexpected medical bill.

If any of this sounds like you, I want you to promise me right now that you're going to shake off any shame or disappointment you might be feeling about the fact that you're in debt.

Forgive yourself for the decisions you've made or the choices you've been forced to make in the past. It may have been because you were backed into a corner. Perhaps you just didn't know any better, because you hadn't been taught financial literacy. Or you were just young and silly – we've all been there, and done things we regret.

What matters now is that you've decided to take charge of your financial security, so let's focus on what you can do from here on out.

Now, back to the question. Can you be in debt and start investing? I'm going to return to my earlier self to answer this question. Remember how I said that back in my early twenties, I'd got myself into debt? I was paying over $850 every month on my personal loans, on top of my rent, bills and discretionary spending.

Which begs the question: how on earth can you invest – or save any money, for that matter – when such a huge chunk of your pay cheque is going towards debt repayment?

Short answer: you can't.

But the way I see it, repaying debt is a form of investing.

Hear me out.

It doesn't make sense to me to invest $100 a month for a 5 per cent return when that money could be put towards paying off debts you owe with interest rates of 9 per cent, 15 per cent, 20 per cent or more.

If you have a personal loan with a 15 per cent interest rate and you pay it off more quickly with extra repayments, then every extra dollar is giving you a return of 15 per cent, as it's interest you won't be paying in the future.

Now, I'm not saying that everyone should take all their savings and funnel it into their debts. For example, I had one friend who had saved $50,000. He was really proud of himself because $50,000 is a lot of money. But he also had $40,000 in credit card debt. He didn't want to use any of his savings to pay down his credit card debt, but with a 20 per cent interest rate, it was costing him around $8,000 a year in interest.

He wasn't interested in starting to pay down the oppressive debt with some of his savings, or at least setting up some sort of consistent payment plan. 'Those savings are my safety net, I'm not touching that account,' he told me. 'If I lose my job, I need to know I have backup to pay the bills.' His approach didn't make the most financial sense but on a more emotional level, driven no doubt by his money story, it really made sense to him.

So, a friendly reminder that there's a duality between the psychological safety net of savings and the burden of debts. Striking the balance is key – and nixing your debts before you start investing is absolutely the ideal way to get started on the front foot.

To help make the best decision about whether you should pay off your debts first or get stuck into investing straightaway, there's one definitive step to take.

And that is to create a budget.

● ●

THE DREADED B-WORD

I know, I know! The word 'budget' might make you feel a bit ick, but I want to take this time to reframe what a budget means, because when you understand where every dollar you earn is going, there are no nasty surprises. It gives you reassurance and freedom to make your own choices.

It's important to live below your means if you want to get ahead in life. That means spending less than you earn, and regularly contributing to savings or investments that will provide security in the future. Creating and sticking to a budget is key, because cash flow is queen!

There's a detailed map on how to do this in *She's on the Money*, but here's a basic breakdown.

First of all, you need to know your current financial position. Start by writing down how much you earn, spend, own and owe right now.

Earn includes any money you have coming in – your salary, Centrelink payments, child support, scholarships, investments. Add it all up.

Spend is your regular outgoings – rent or mortgage, utility bills, subscriptions, car-related expenses, food and entertainment.

....

Own covers your assets – this includes your super balance, money in your savings account, and the equity you have in your home, if you own one.

....

Owe is your debts – credit cards, personal loans, car loans, buy now, pay later, HECS and mortgage. Some of this already counts as investment debt in my book – HECS that's helped you into a great career, or a mortgage for a property that's increased in value.

....

So . . . how does it look? Do you owe more than you own? Do your expenses outstrip your income?

- If not, great! Sounds like you could be in a great position to start investing.
- If your answer is yes, that's still okay. Keep reading, so you can learn the ins and outs of investing, and consider referring back to *She's on the Money* to get your budget and cash flow on track.

● ●

WHEN ALL ELSE FAILS, GO BACK TO YOUR VALUES

If you're looking over your budget and fretting a bit, wondering how you can possibly cut out a single thing, try reframing the question from the perspective of what really matters to you.

Can't imagine giving up your fortnightly girls' night with friends, where you each spend $100 on cocktails and a fancy meal? Ask yourself: is it the cocktails and canapés you can't give up? Or is it the quality time with your pals? Because you can still have that on a budget.

Why not take it in turns hosting at home? If one friend cooks each time and you BYO alcohol, you could slash that $100 to $25, and still get a side of juicy gossip – for free!

• •

INVESTING ON AN IRREGULAR INCOME

There are lots of reasons why someone might be on an irregular income. Maybe you're a student and you only work minimal hours when classes are running but pick up extra shifts during semester breaks. You might work for yourself, or as a subcontractor, and go weeks or months without getting paid before the cash from several invoices floods in. Shift work, penalty rates and rotating rosters can also mean your fortnightly or monthly pay fluctuates.

One of the easiest ways to manage a variable income is to take a step back and look at the bigger picture. If you know how much you're likely to earn for the entire year (checking last year's tax return can help you figure this out), then you can average out your earnings and come up with a number that you should have to potentially invest. You can 'pay' yourself this amount, allowing any extra to build up in a different account to cover you for those periods when you don't have as much coming in.

Once you have your average earnings, take a look at your bank statements for the past 12 months. Tally up how much you spend on utilities and subscriptions, rent or mortgage, transport, food and entertainment, add a buffer of 5 or 10 per cent to account for any changes or miscalculations, then divide that by the number of pay periods in a year – 52 weeks, 26 fortnights, or 12 months.

Now, subtract your expenses from your average income for the same period. What's left is what you could potentially use to invest.

Average earnings = ...

Utilities and subscriptions = ...

Rent/mortgage = ...

Transport = ...

Food and entertainment = ...

Any other expenses = ...

Buffer (5 or 10 per cent) = ...

Divided by pay periods in year = ...

Average income minus expenses (per pay period) = ...

● ●

Beware lifestyle creep

Lifestyle creep is when our discretionary spending increases as our income goes up. So we're earning more money, but we don't seem to have anything to show for it at the end of the month.

You get a pay rise, and you're immediately thinking about how much this will boost your savings, how you'll magically have that extra $10,000 minus tax sitting in your bank account at the end of the financial year, and how it'll bring you so much closer to your financial goals. Your new and improved pay will go in and *voila*! A whole hunk of cash just sitting there, waiting for you. Right?

Wrong!

Even the most frugal among us tend to unconsciously increase our spending when our income improves. We don't mean to, but it happens! It could be something as small as not automatically choosing the supermarket own brand for your kitchen staples, or buying a $20 bottle of wine instead of the $12.99 special.

These aren't huge, expensive changes – it's not like you're going out and buying a new car or a pair of diamond earrings or something – but over the year, they add up. One dollar extra for a tin of tomatoes here, a cheeky $30 on Uber Eats because you can't be bothered cooking there . . . before you know it, your entire pay rise has been swallowed up by lifestyle creep.

I'm not suggesting you don't splurge on yourself ever, at all! It's fine for you to treat or reward yourself, but that spending should be intentional. It's when the lifestyle creep and additional spending is unintentional that it can become really problematic.

One way to avoid lifestyle creep is to commit to always saving or investing a portion of any pay increase you receive, so it's not just sitting there, waiting for you to spend. At least half should be put to good use, not frittered away.

An example is if a pay rise works out to be $200 per week after tax, set up a direct transfer to your savings account of $120. There's still an extra $80 to spend without losing it all to lifestyle creep.

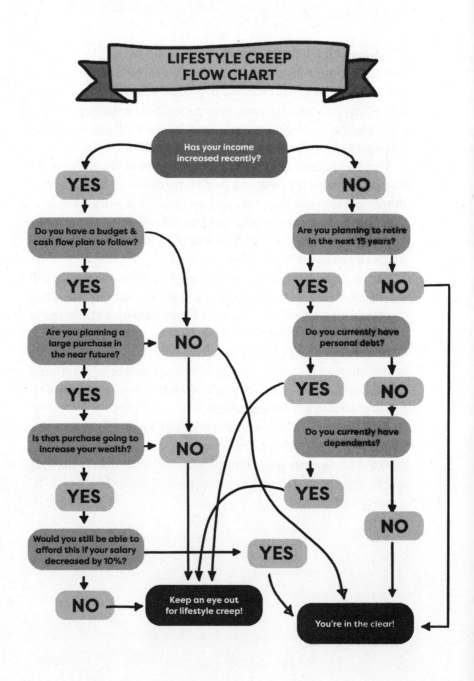

LIFESTYLE CREEP
FLOW CHART

Has your income increased recently?

YES

NO

Do you have a budget & cash flow plan to follow?

Are you planning to retire in the next 15 years?

YES

YES   NO

Are you planning a large purchase in the near future?

NO

Do you currently have personal debt?

YES

YES   NO

Is that purchase going to increase your wealth?

NO

Do you currently have dependents?

YES

YES

Would you still be able to afford this if your salary decreased by 10%?

YES

NO

NO

Keep an eye out for lifestyle creep!

You're in the clear!

Emergency! Emergency!

I can't write this chapter without including this not-so-sexy but oh-so-important bit – the emergency fund. This is non-negotiable, and one of the very first things I want you to set up before you start investing.

There's a couple of reasons why absolutely everyone on the planet should do whatever they can do to build up an emergency fund.

First is . . . well, for an actual emergency, obviously. Car dies, cat needs surgery, roof blows off in a storm. Your emergency fund should be at least enough to cover your insurance excess, plus a buffer, for these types of things.

Another reason is so that you're not forced into a terrible financial choice, such as selling your shares at a loss, or walking away from an investment with nothing.

How much should your emergency fund be? Again, there's no clear-cut answer to this one. For some people it might be $500; others couldn't imagine feeling comfortable with less than $50,000.

A good rule of thumb is that your emergency fund should be able to cover three months' worth of your day-to-day expenses – not luxuries, just the bare necessities like food, rent, electricity and petrol. This number will change as your circumstances change. You'll probably need to increase it if you buy a home or have kids, for example.

'But Victoria, how am I supposed to start an emergency fund when I don't have a few thousand bucks just lying around?'

Here are a few ideas:

- Take on some extra shifts at work, or get an evening/weekend job.
- Start a side hustle – babysitting, freelancing, Uber-something.

- Sell some of your clutter (think: clothes, bags, shoes, etc.) on Facebook Marketplace, Gumtree, eBay or Depop.
- Shop around for discounts on insurance, utilities and subscriptions, and channel the savings into your emergency account.
- Use your tax return, Medicare rebates or annual bonus to build it up.

Repeat after me: I will not spend/dip into/invest my emergency fund.

It will remain intact until it is needed for AN EMERGENCY. Flights to Bali or that big designer sale are NOT AN EMERGENCY. Not even if it's a once-in-a-lifetime bargain!

I also want to stress how important it is to have access to your own emergency fund, even if you're in a relationship. Even if you can't imagine things going bad between you and your partner, you still need access to your own stash of cash.

Why? Well, there are the obvious reasons, such as your partner turns out to be absolutely awful and ends up hurting you, cheating on you or revealing a gambling/drug/alcohol problem they've kept well-hidden. Some people call it their Fuck Off Fund – money they can access if they need to do a midnight bolt.

But there are also situations that would never occur to most people. For example, if you only have joint accounts and something terrible (God forbid) happens to your other half, what would you do if your bank froze the accounts? What if your sister desperately needed your help in a financial emergency, but she didn't want your partner to know?

The other thing an emergency fund gives you is the power to say no. Hate your boss so much that getting out of bed and dragging yourself to work every day is pure torture? It gives you the power to quit. Stuck with a partner who treats you like crap, but can't afford the rent without their wage? It gives you the power to tell them where to go.

Worst-case scenario, if you never end up needing it for an actual emergency, then woohoo, bonus money! But please make it a priority to start building your emergency fund today, even if it's just $20 a week to start. You'll never regret it – and I really don't want you to look back and regret *not* doing it.

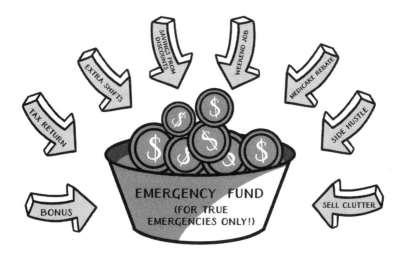

Estate planning

This goes hand-in-hand with the emergency fund. If you don't have kids yet, estate planning probably isn't something you've really thought about, but you should start thinking about it now, especially with all that wealth we're about to build through investing!

You need to have a will in place – even a basic one will do – so that you have control over where your assets go if anything was to happen to you. Seriously, make an appointment with a lawyer and get it sorted. I don't love those DIY wills you can get from the post office, but they're better than nothing if you can't afford to go the whole way with an estate lawyer right now.

'But Victoria, surely estate planning is only an issue for the mega-rich who have millions to allocate to various family members?'

That couldn't be further from the truth!

Don't you want to know that your hard-earned assets will go to the right people? And surely the last thing you want is your loved ones fighting it out in court when you're gone? If you die without a valid will in place, what's called 'dying intestate', the law determines who your assets are distributed to, no matter your personal wishes or situation.

Chat to anyone who's been through the process of dealing with someone's finances when they've passed away without a will, and ask them what hoops they've had to jump through just to sort out the inheritance.

One of the best things you can do for your family (or friends, if that's who you'll be leaving your assets to) is to ensure they won't need to go through all of that while they're still grieving their loss. Whether your estate is worth $1,000, $10,000 or $10 million, saving them that stress and heartache is priceless.

Your will needs to include details of where all your assets will go – super, cash in the bank, properties, insurance payouts, any valuable items such as cars, antiques or jewellery – plus how your children or pets will be cared for, and how this will be paid for.

You might also want to include certain conditions, such as how old your kids need to be before they receive a big cash payout, or if the money is earmarked for specific things, such as school fees or their first home.

One final thought: estate planning is not a set-and-forget kind of thing. You'll need to reassess it if you begin a new relationship, get divorced, have kids, acquire or dispose of big assets and when you retire. As your assets and investments become more complicated, I strongly suggest getting professional help to make sure it's done correctly.

What's the saying again? Hope for the best, plan for the worst.

Superannuation, investing, and the power of compound interest

They say the best time to invest was ten years ago and the next best time is today. Every extra day, month or year you remain invested increases the opportunity your money has to grow.

Why? Because of the magic of compound interest.

Compound interest sounds complicated, but it's actually pretty simple. The basic premise of compound interest is that any interest you earn is added to your principal balance, so the following period, you're earning interest on a higher balance than the one before.

Each year, the interest keeps accruing (compounding), acting kind of like a snowball gathering momentum as it speeds downhill.

Let's say you have $100, and it will earn 10 per cent compound interest each year. The first year, you'll earn $10.

The following year, you'll still be earning 10 per cent interest, but this time, it will be on $110 – so you'll earn $11. The year after that, your interest will be $12.10 (10 per cent of $121), and so on.

Compound interest means that even if you never add to that money again, it will continue to grow, and grow, and grow.

Take this example.

Let's say you put $5,000 into super at the age of 23. That's all you put in, and you never touch that super account again; you don't add any more money, or subtract anything.

Over time, investment returns will go up and down, but assuming a balanced investment return rate of an average of 5 per cent per annum (after fees), your $5,000 will be worth around $40,650 by the time you're 65. Remember, that's without you topping up the account at all along the way!

If you add an extra $100 a month from the age of 23, that investment grows to $211,790 by 65.

This is real money that has the ability to pay for your life in retirement, and Every. Little. Bit. Counts.

And the sooner you get started, the better.

• • • • • •

CARRIE, 41 – QLD

My super provides good returns, which aligns with my values. And they provide me with options for insurance should I need to claim. The insurance is important to me as I was diagnosed with cancer in 2019, and now I can still claim should the worst happen and I need to. It's peace of mind. I think this is something I will reassess once I am five years cancer-free, which is when you are considered cured. It's also really important for mental health knowing that these options are available.

JESS, 27 – NSW

I invested in property when I was very young as I had saved a good chunk of money and wanted to do something with it. After seeing my parents struggle, I didn't want to worry, and being in an unpredictable industry, I wanted to feel secure. It is not making me money (month-to-month), but I know the rent is helping to pay off the mortgage so I will have equity to buy my own home one day. I have a budget and it's not very strict due to my variable income, but I have a system each week when I get paid, where I pay all my expenses and transfer the rest into my offset account. My offset acts as my emergency account and savings.

• • • • • •

TAKE NOTE

It's important to understand your current financial position before you start investing. My view is that even paying off debt is a form of investing in Future You.

....

We budget for the things we need, the things we want and the things we don't even want to think about. Each is as important as the others.

....

Chapter 5

An introduction to investing

Now, class, I'm going to give you a teeny tiny history lesson because how investing actually came about is something hardly any of us were ever taught in school. (Or maybe I'd just snuck off to go shopping that day . . . ?)

Investing has been around literally forever – we're talking from ancient Mesopotamia through to medieval and Renaissance Europe. But the share market in the form that we currently recognise first came to life around 1600, with the Amsterdam Stock Exchange. Then lots happened during the 1700s and 1800s, especially in the US, with pension funds coming into existence and the beginning of the modern banking industry. You might have heard of the Dow Jones, a stock index that allows people to gauge how the market is performing, which popped up in the 1800s. Also around this time a company was founded that became Standard & Poor's (great name, right?), a credit agency that among many other things is the creator of the

S&P 500 Index. (I mention this because it'll come up again later in the book so you'll thank me then!) The S&P 500 is probably the most popular equity index in the world and it is used to benchmark the performance of some of America's biggest companies. It's a key indicator of market health, which is why people refer to it a lot.

Meanwhile, here in Australia, investing has been going on since the early days of European settlement. The first company was founded in the colony of New South Wales in 1817, called the Bank of New South Wales – we now know it as Westpac!

The Australian Stock Exchange Limited (ASX) was formed on 1 April 1987 (so it's still pretty young) and it brought together the six independent, state-based stock exchanges.

Then, in 2006, the Australian Stock Exchange merged with the Sydney Futures Exchange and changed its name (but, conveniently, not the acronym) to the Australian Securities Exchange, to reflect the new, more diverse range of products.

Hot tip: A good local index to know about is the All Ordinaries share price index (SPI), introduced in 1983 (ever heard someone mention the 'All Ords' and drawn a blank? This is what they were talking about!). Basically, it tracks the 500 largest companies listed on the ASX.

'But Victoria, I don't get why any of this is relevant to me?'

I hear you – it's a little dry! The main point I'd like you to take away is that throughout recessions and depressions, share market crashes, world wars, the Asian Financial Crisis, the Global Financial Crisis and the rise of the internet, share markets have weathered every storm. That's a good thing to remember when markets are looking a bit volatile and scary in the short term. The other bonus is, with most countries now having their own share markets, we can invest all over the world thanks to international brokers. Sweet!

TICKER CODES, AND HOW THEY WORK

The ASX issues a unique ticker code to each exchange-traded product, which identifes the type of product it is, so people aren't misled into investing in things they don't understand.

Different types of products have different coding conventions. For example:

- **Ordinary shares on the ASX market** – the first character of the code usually matches the first character of the name of the company or trust; for example, Apple's code is AAPL, Nike's is NYSE and Amazon's is AMZN.
- **Exchange traded funds (ETFs)** – usually have a three- or four-character code that reflects the name of the fund; for example, the code for the S&P 500 (which is an index so can't be bought or sold, only reported) is ^GSPC. Structured products and single asset funds have a six-character code, with the first three characters reflecting the name of the fund.
- **Warrants** – have a six-character code. The first three characters represent the underlying instrument. The remaining characters indicate the type of warrant, issuer and series.
- **Australian government bonds** – these codes start with GSB or GSI.
- **Interest rate securities** – these codes consist of three characters indicating the issuer, followed by character/s identifying the type of security and maturity.[10]

What are the different investment types?

Okay, history class dismissed! Now let's dive into the juicy details of what it really means to invest.

When we think about different types of investments and what works best for our current situation, goals and risk tolerance, we need to consider three main things:

- **Volatility** – how much could the price of the asset vary?
- **Capital** – how much will it cost you? What's the initial outlay?
- **Liquidity** – what happens if you need access to this money in a hurry? How quickly and easily can you convert the asset back into cold hard cash?

With all that in mind, here are a few of the main types of investments.

Cash

We all know what cash is, whether it's in your transaction account, a term deposit or a savings account. It's relatively secure and accessible, for quick access if needed. It's relatively low risk, with low volatility, and provided you have it in the bank earning a teeny bit of interest, it will produce a regular (albeit very low) income.

The main trouble with cash is that your returns are loooooow, and because any income you do make is taxable, you're automatically losing a percentage of whatever piddly interest you're earning. Cash is a bit like one of those giant tortoises that live for a hundred years – they move super-slow, but they keep trudging forward, and their big shell makes them almost indestructible.

Property

I would class property as a medium-security asset. You can earn a regular income from rent and you can insure property against damage or loss. The main thing people find attractive about property is that it's tangible. You can reach out and touch it – it's real. Over the longer term, land prices grow in value, and you can leverage your equity to buy more properties or to renovate. Your equity is the difference between what your property is currently worth and how much you have left owing on the loan, and can be used as security with banks and lenders. However, it's worth noting that not all of your equity might be useable; banks typically allow you to lend 80 per cent of your property's value less the debt you still owe against it.

Property is commonly known as an illiquid asset. As I've said before, you can't simply slice off a room when you need a few thousand dollars, and there may be maintenance and upkeep that perhaps you didn't expect. If you do decide to sell, there are advertising and agents' fees to consider, and you really have no idea how much a property is worth until it's sold.

And while, yes, you can make an income from rent, this is highly dependent upon demand. If the area or property type is not popular, you won't be able to charge a premium price.

Property is such a diverse asset class in itself, I'd liken it to dogs – some are dependable, like golden retrievers; others are like yappy little chihuahuas. They talk a big game but fail to deliver when it comes to the crunch. Others again are like English bulldogs, and perhaps seem amazing at first glance, but may come with all these hidden issues that cost you loads of money and stress.

And just like choosing a dog, you need to choose the property type, location and strategy that's right for you. You might even realise that dogs (or property) are not right for you at all, and you want another pet (or strategy) altogether.

Bonds and fixed interest assets

Fixed interest assets are relatively secure assets which offer consistent returns over a specified time period. This means you'll receive regular income at set interest rates, and they won't fluctuate like other asset classes. You could also get a higher return than you would on cash in the bank, without really flexing your risk-tolerating muscles too much.

A bond is a fixed interest asset that you can view as a loan made by an investor to a borrower, which is typically a corporate organisation or the government. You've probably heard of bonds before because they're one of the asset classes that individual investors are fairly familiar with alongside shares, cash and property. I like to look at bonds as an IOU – but a more serious, legitimate one, not the kind written in primary school when your friend bought you a snack at the canteen!

Bonds are your slow and steady old horse, clip-clopping away at a reliable pace, unlikely to buck you off anytime soon. In return for lending your money, you receive coupon payments (basically regular interest payments) and then you get the face value of the bond back at the end of the specified term period if you've kept the bond the whole time (i.e. until 'maturity').

There are a few different options when investing in bonds and just like every other asset class, each option carries its own sets of risks and potential return. The two main types of bonds you can invest in are:

→ **Corporate bonds:** these types of bond are usually part of a public offer, where a business issues an opportunity and individual investors are able to make a direct investment into that business.

→ **Australian government bonds:** corporate government securities or CGS are issued directly by the Australian government. These can be bought through your chosen trading platform or directly through the ASX. The value of an Australian government bond is fixed along with its interest rate, and payments are generally made to you every three to six months until the end of your bond term, when your initial investment is returned. Government bonds tend to be relatively lower risk than corporate ones.

In addition to credit risk relating to the issuer, the value of a bond can increase or even decrease over time before your bond term expires based on current interest rates. If you've invested in a bond with a floating rate, if interest rates drop, you will likely see an increase in the value of your bonds, and if interest rates rise, the value of your bonds will usually drop. Whereas if you've opted for a fixed rate bond, its value won't change.

In terms of historical returns, the Australian bonds return rate has been 7.6 per cent per annum since 1 January 1970 and 5.1 per cent per annum since 1 January 2000.[11]

Generally, bonds issued in the primary market are not available to individual investors and they can cost five or six figures apiece. So instead, what usually happens is institutional investors buy the bonds directly and then break them down into smaller parcels for sale to investors (like you or me!) via the secondary market. In this way, similar to shares, you can invest in bond products via the ASX, for as little as 1 cent depending on which platform you choose! Another option is investing in the bond market through exchange traded funds (ETFs) or exchange traded bonds, which can be bought and sold on a stock exchange through an online trading platform or a broker. For example, bonds with a floating rate are harder for the average investor to invest in directly as they're usually only offered to institutional investors, but they can be accessed via an ETF.

If you really need to get back your money that you've invested in bonds, it is possible; however, if you sell them before maturity you'll get their market value back (which could be higher or lower than the face value that you'd get back if you held them until maturity).

Listed shares

Many people think shares are a high-risk game, and they are defined as a high-risk asset, but they are much less scary than you might believe. Shares in large companies are usually highly liquid, which means you can sell some or all at any given time. If the company grows, your capital also grows, you might earn an income if it's a company that issues dividends to its shareholders, and you can check the value whenever you like.

However, shares can be volatile, and you are at risk of having your investment go backwards if things turn sour. There's also the information overload factor – so much jargon, so many numbers, and so many armchair experts giving you tips, it can feel like your head is going to explode! Some people see shares a bit like an exotic big cat – sleek, sexy, exciting, but unpredictable. You need to build up a strong relationship with them over time, and keep your eye on them so they don't turn around and bite you when you least expect it!

Hot tip: Nowadays, shares and stocks are terms used pretty interchangeably, though 'stock' is more in use in the US, and Australia and the UK tend to go with 'share'. Also, stock can refer to the broad idea of ownership in a company, where a share is the exact amount of ownership: 'I own stock' versus 'I own a share'.

WHAT'S THE DIFFERENCE BETWEEN SHARES AND BONDS?

Great question, so glad you asked! With shares it's easier to access your money, whereas bonds are locked in for a period. With shares you're an owner (part-owner of the company you've bought the shares in), and with bonds you're a lender (you have loaned the government or company the money). And if a company collapses, its bondholders are paid out before its shareholders.

So, how do people actually make money in the share market?

This is another question I field quite a lot and it's certainly not a dumb one!

There are two key factors at play when it comes to making money on the share market.

The first is to invest with regularity and consistency. *How much* you contribute isn't nearly as important as *how regularly* you contribute.

The second factor is time. With enough time on your side, even small, regular contributions can result in huge gains down the track.

While many people view the share market as a terrifying, volatile beast, this is only true if you're looking at shares on a day-to-day or month-to-month basis. When you take a step back and look at the bigger picture, taking into account growth over a 30-year period, you gain a different perspective.

Take a squiz at this graph, which tracks the value of the ASX 200 since 1990. Can you see how, despite all the little bumps that would look more extreme close up, it's still ultimately trended upwards?

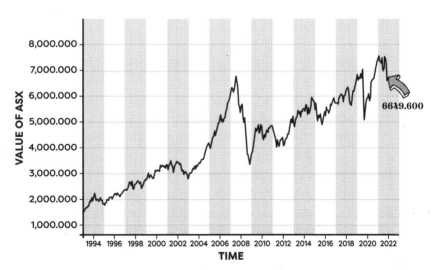

01 Jan 1990 – 19 July 2022
Past performance does not guarantee future performance.
(Source: Yahoo Finance.)

If you're looking to make a quick buck and you're jumping in and out of different shares? Sure, you're vulnerable. If you've put all your eggs in one basket and only invested in one or two particular shares? Yes, even over the long term you run the risk of those shares stagnating or going backwards – which is why a diversified approach is so key. But if you have your money in a portfolio of quality investments, you contribute regularly, and you leave it invested for a longer period? That's a different story.

Literally anyone can create wealth this way because, like I said, you don't have to be funnelling thousands of dollars every month towards your investments. If you're a single parent and only working part-time, $20 or $50 invested regularly and consistently can still provide a return over a long period.

You don't need to start out with a huge wad of cash either. The key is spending less than you earn (i.e. avoiding debt) and investing over the longer term.

'But Victoria, I still don't get how people actually make money through the share market?'

This happens in two ways: through capital growth, and dividends.

Capital growth means the share price has increased over time. You buy shares at $1.10 each, and now they're worth $1.50 each – that's capital growth of 40c per share.

Dividends are your share of the earnings or retained profits the company has decided to share with its shareholders. You can keep these dividends as savings or reinvest them.

What I'm looking for personally when I'm investing in shares, as a relatively high-risk investor, is that they have a higher dividend yield, which could signal they're improving over time (although I'd cross-check that against the general health of the company). You can calculate the dividend yield of a particular company by dividing the annual dividend per share by the share price.

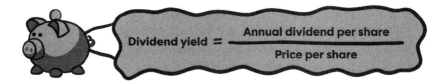

$$\text{Dividend yield} = \frac{\text{Annual dividend per share}}{\text{Price per share}}$$

WHAT ARE FRANKING CREDITS?

Franking credits are distributed to shareholders (i.e. investors) at the same time as dividend payments, by eligible Australian-resident companies that pay income tax. Because these companies have already paid tax, when they distribute their after-tax profits by way of franked dividends, these franked dividends have franking credits attached to them. This means you generally should pay less income tax on the dividends when you process your own tax return (you might even be entitled to a refund depending on your tax rate). In short, the arrangement helps eliminate the double taxation of dividends.

Now, I'm sorry to burst some bubbles here, but the best shares with the highest dividend yields are not your glitzy, glamorous or exciting companies that have huge amounts of capital growth, like Afterpay or Uber. The shares that everyone's talking about around the water cooler that are going gangbusters over a short time aren't your high dividend yield shares.

The shares that tend to consistently pay the highest dividends are those bog-standard, boring investments that your grand-parents would feel comfortable with – blue chip stocks that plod along, growing slowly but consistently over the longer term, paying out regular dividends.

Figuring out the right mix of high capital growth and high divi-dend yield investments depends on your risk appetite, life stage and goals. It also depends on your income and tax strategy, because you'll only pay tax on capital growth when you sell your shares, whereas dividend yields will increase your taxable income (and the tax you'll need to pay) for that financial year.

You may be looking for more regular dividend income, you may be wanting more capital growth – and this may change as your life circumstances evolve and you have kids, buy a house, or retire.

Whatever your goals with your share investments, here is something to keep in mind. This chart shows the performance of different asset classes since 1990:

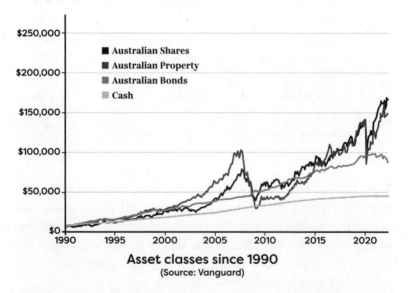

Asset classes since 1990
(Source: Vanguard)

I don't want you to focus on which asset class is the best performer, because this varies over time and past performance doesn't always indicate future performance.

However, if you look to the left of the chart, you'll see that if you invest for ten years or longer, you may not actually lose anything by investing. Where you lose money is if you get caught up in the volatility of the market and you panic and sell.

The crash in 2009 looks large, but if you look further across the chart, you can see the market's recovered (and then some). COVID had a significant impact too – however, just like every dips that has been experienced in the share market, at the time of writing prices have started to bounce back as the world begins to settle.

To give you some perspective, every other little drop in earlier years was also when a big crash occurred. But time has made the crashes look smaller now. The important thing to see is that those who invest over the long term are less likely to lose money. It's those who crystallise their losses by leaving the market for whatever reason who end up with losses.

What on earth is a bear market? And a bull market?

Essentially, a bull market is one that's raring to go – like a bull. Full of optimism and excitement, characterised by rising stock prices and a strong economy.

A bear market, by contrast, is one that is receding, like a bear going into hibernation. Stocks are declining in value and the economy isn't looking so rosy.

Hot tip: another easy way to remember this is by how each animal attacks – bulls scoop their opponent up with their horns, while bears swipe downwards to crush their opponent to the ground. As far as I'm concerned, both sound awful and I would not want to get into an argument with either animal, thanks very much!

BULL MARKET VERSUS BEAR MARKET

SWIPES UP
WHEN
ATTACKING

SWIPES DOWN
WHEN
ATTACKING

BULL MARKET

- OPTIMISM
- PRICES GOING UP

BEAR MARKET

- PESSIMISM
- PRICES GOING DOWN

Some investors try to use this distinction to 'time the market' – that is, invest low and sell high. But it's impossible to accurately predict when the market will 'bottom out'. If I could do it, I'd be on my private island, eating lobster encrusted with gold leaf, with a team of people to count up all my money!

Thanks to the media and the well-meaning 'expertise' of friends and family, lots of people get caught up in what's going on in the market and forget that the key to success is consistent investment over the longer term. So please don't get yourself too wound up about whether we're experiencing a bull or bear market at any point in time – remember, you're in it for the long haul. At the end of the day, if you're investing for 20, 30 or 40 years, these minor fluctuations don't matter.

So my (general) advice is to file these terms away in your glossary, but don't worry too much about how they impact your investments.

What is inflation, and how does it impact my investments?

Inflation refers to the trend of increased prices and cost of living across the economy as a whole, over time. Think of it like a $2 coin you've found in an old piggy bank. Back when you were eight, you could have bought heaps of lollies or a huge ice cream. Today, though, you'd be lucky to get a chocolate bar for the same price. Today, $2 simply doesn't buy what it did ten or 20 years ago.

Inflation is important because even if you're growing your wealth through investments, you're only growing your wealth in real terms if the growth is surpassing inflation.

If the cost of a chocolate bar is going up 8 per cent each year and your investments are only increasing by 7 per cent, you're actually able to buy less with that money as the years go on – so you're going backwards, even though it seems like your wealth is increasing.

This is why keeping cash in the bank isn't always the best way to preserve your wealth. What kind of interest rate are you earning on your savings account right now?

As long as inflation is increasing by more than that each year, you are technically losing money by allowing it to sit in the bank. Your wealth is actually being eroded by inflation. Rude, isn't it?

When we invest, we're looking for assets that will grow at a rate that exceeds inflation.

Again, please don't focus on the monthly or even yearly figures – this is a long-term process. But it is important to understand how inflation works, and how it impacts your investments, so you don't end up treading water, or worse – drowning in the increased cost of living.

Another reason inflation is so important is that when you're planning for how much money you'll require in retirement, you need to be looking at how much things will cost in the future. It's no good saying you can live comfortably on $80,000 today, so

$80,000 in retirement, once you've paid your mortgage off, will be heaps. Bread won't cost the same 30 years from now as it does today. Neither will almond milk, avocados or organic kombucha. You'll need an income that can support these purchases at the price tags they'll have when you retire.

Hot tip: The easiest way to calculate the target figure that will cover what you think you'll need and also account for inflation is to use an online calculator that does it for you. Save yourself a headache! There are a few good ones out there.

A note on cryptocurrency

Remember that list at the start of this chapter, of the different asset classes? Do you remember seeing crypto on there? No? I wonder why . . .

Well, crypto isn't actually regarded as an asset class in Australia. That's why it's not on that list. At the time of writing, financial advisers can't give advice on it. That's because it currently doesn't have the stability or longevity that other asset classes, like shares and property, have. It's not completely regulated by ASIC either, which in my view should be a huge red flag.

The value of any cryptocurrency is wholly reliant on the value that society currently puts on it. It's based on a pack mentality – a really volatile, psychologically driven phenomenon that we can't properly quantify – and it's full of animosity. If you're wanting crypto information, I'm not your gal and this isn't the book for you. I get that it's new and exciting, but its long-term performance is also unproven – and I'm all about calculated risks with a long-term time frame, not jumping off into the deep end with no life jacket.

Personal advice or general advice – which is right for me?

We're all looking for personalised advice tailored to our unique situation. Whether it's how to get fit or organise our home, whenever we're reading a book or a blog, or listening to a podcast, we're searching for those titbits that apply particularly to ourselves.

However, all of these things – this book included – are actually general advice.

When you're listening to a podcast, surfing Facebook groups or skimming through the latest financial bestseller (maybe the one you're holding right now!), I know what you're hoping for. You want something to pop out at you that says, 'Hey, here's the solution to your exact problem! This is precisely what you should do, step by step.'

The reality is, it's neither possible nor ethical for any author or content creator to do that.

We can only give broad-based, general advice because we have absolutely no way of knowing anything about our readers or listeners. We don't know if you're $100,000 in debt or if you've just inherited more money than you can count. We don't know your salary, lifestyle, commitments, values or risk tolerance, so we can't guarantee that any tips, tricks or advice we have to offer will suit you.

For example, I couldn't say on my podcast that if you have a spare $50,000 lying around, the best thing to do with it would be to invest it in bonds or the share market. For some people, this would be great advice. But for others, such as those who need to access the money soon for a house deposit, it could be terrible advice!

Personal advice, on the other hand, takes all this into account; your current position and goals, what values and ethics are close to your heart, your age and your risk tolerance.

That's why no general advice – not even this super awesome book! – can ever replace the tailored advice you receive from a financial adviser. They'll have you complete a FactFind, meet with you in person or online to understand you better, and go through any relevant documentation such as insurance policies, superannuation statements and investments.

All of these things are like pieces of the puzzle that, when an adviser puts them all together, form your personalised financial advice.

● ● ● ● ● ●

CONNIE, 39 – NSW

I receive shares as part of my employee benefits each year which I reinvest my dividends in to buy more shares. I also take part in any employee share offers and buy them usually at a discounted rate. I have also started using micro-investing platforms thanks to SOTM I think of shares as a set-and-forget method of investing as I am not planning on touching or using those funds for many years.

STEPH, 24 – NSW

My money story has changed a lot in the last year. I left the company I was starting with friends and got a full-time job, and now that I have a relatively stable income, I'm working towards creating a realistic budget each week. I've also started investing, which has made me less stressed for the future. Yes, I may have a bit less money in short term savings, a holiday fund or even to splurge on a night out, but knowing I'm investing in my financial future down the track makes it worth it! The biggest blocker for me was that I was worried about not having a 'big' amount of savings readily accessible, but I've slowly realised over the last 18 months that there is no reason to have tens of thousands in a savings account, not accruing much interest and just sitting there.

● ● ● ● ● ●

TAKE NOTE

Make sure you consider an asset's volatility, capital
and liquidity before you start investing.

....

You don't need thousands of dollars to invest;
the key is regularity and consistency.

....

While general advice is a good way to get started, it can't ever
replace personal advice that you get from a financial adviser.

....

Chapter 6

A deep dive into shares

You're now a little more informed and perhaps intrigued at the idea of investing in shares. You might be thinking about what kinds of shares you could invest in down the track. Or maybe you're absolutely frothing about the idea of starting a share port-folio immediately, if not sooner?

Whatever your interest level, here's the thing about investing in shares: it rarely pays to dive in first and do your research later.

Now we're going to dissect some of the nitty-gritty ins and outs of shares, from the different ways you can make money in the share market to the terminology that had you scratching your head in the past.

First things first. At a really basic level: why do shares exist?

The entire purpose of a company being on the ASX is to raise money. Being on the share market enables companies to raise capital, which they use to invest in systems, people, processes, projects and plans, with a goal of ultimately growing their business and making a bigger profit.

Investors are the people who give that money to that company. As a share investor, you choose to give your money to a company because you believe that its stock is going to be more valuable in the future than it is now and in return you get a tiny piece of the company and a share in its profits.

Straight up, I'm going to talk you through some of the different terms and phrases to do with share investing, including the different types of shares, what they mean and how they work.

Ordinary share and preferred share

There are two common types of shares: ordinary and preferred.

Ordinary shares are readily available and easy to buy. If you own an ordinary share, you have minority voting rights and you may potentially earn dividends.

Preferred shares are issued a bit like a bond. They're not necessarily commonly available and if you own a preferred share, you basically get to call 'dibs' on the dividends. Most preferred shares have a fixed dividend, while ordinary shares generally don't. This means that if and when dividends are paid, as the owner of a preferred share, you'll get paid first. If the company goes bankrupt, you'll usually get paid out before the rest of the ordinary shareholders (after any debts are repaid).

Sounds like a massive win, right? With all of those benefits, why would you ever choose an ordinary share over a preferred one?

As always, there's a catch. In exchange for this VIP status, preferred shareholders typically don't hold any voting rights or their rights are limited. This is a sit-down-and-shut-up style of investing.

Neither of these types of shares are 'better' or 'worse' than the other. The right type for you will depend on your values and how involved and active you want to be with your share portfolio.

What is a share buyback?

A buyback happens when the company doesn't want to have shareholders, or as many shareholders, anymore.

This can be for a range of reasons. A company might initially issue shares in order to raise capital then later decide to buy them back in order to regain a greater level of control from shareholders – they realise, 'Hey! We're a really profitable, strong business now. We want to own more of our own business again.' A recent example: Elon Musk was going to buy Twitter and Twitter planned to implement a US$44 billion buyback so it could go private. Or a company might have surplus cash and choose to re-invest in itself by buying back some shares. Sometimes it's to improve the company's ratio of debt to equity, changing the capital structure.

A share buyback results in an overall reduction in the total number of a company's shares on issue. If it has 10,000 shares issued and offers to buy back 2,000 shares, there are now only 8,000 outstanding shares in the market. Thanks to market dynamics, this generally raises the price of those shares and boosts the return to their shareholders, because the company's profit will be spread across fewer shares, improving the earnings per share ratio. So it's also a way of lifting share values as well as improving returns for shareholders, which many companies cite as one of their main objectives.

What is a share split?

A share split is when a company wants to increase how many shares it has in the market to make them appear more affordable. If you bought two shares in a company worth $100 each and they issue a 2-for-1 share split, you now have four shares in the company worth $50 each.

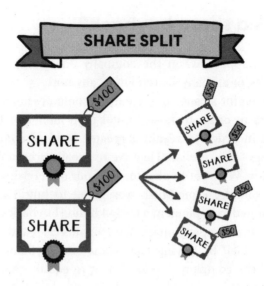

Do you know who loves a share split? Apple. They are massive fans. They've done this multiple times.

- June 1987: 2-for-1 split
- June 2000: 2-for-1 split
- February 2005: 2-for-1 split
- June 2014: 7-for-1 split
- August 2020: 4-for-1 split

At their August 2020 share split, the average Apple share was worth around US$500. At the time of writing, it's worth around US$165. It split by four and $165 x 4 equals $660, so Apple shares have effectively increased in value since its last share split.

Why does Apple do this? One of the most often cited reasons for the Apple share splits is that it encourages new investors, by creating more accessible (i.e. more affordable) shares. A split share is often a sign that a company is thriving, as its share price has increased – and while that's a really good thing, it means shares become less affordable for new investors. So the company may do a share split to make it more affordable and enticing to investors.

Apple stock has significantly increased in value over the last four decades, and if they hadn't issued share splits over the years, by 2021 a single Apple share would have been worth around US$1,800.[12] By doing share splits, they've kept liquidity high and ensured their share price remains affordable and accessible to smaller investors, so the barrier to entry stays low. At the same time, the diversification of their shareholders mitigates their risk as a company.

You know how I love to bring all this money stuff back to psychology? Well, that's also at play with share splits. Firstly because a newly lower share price for a desirable stock like Apple is very appealing to traders and investors, and might tempt them to buy out of natural instinct. And secondly because by splitting stock, a company sends the signal that it's performing well, and that helps build momentum in the market.

Growth share versus dividend share

A share could be both a growth and a dividend share, but it's more likely to be one or the other.

Growth shares aim to benefit shareholders through capital appreciation. As a growth investor, you will purchase a growth share if you feel it will significantly increase in price over time. The main purpose of a growth share is to grow in value.

For instance: if you bought an Apple share in 2007, you would have paid around US$3–6 for the equivalent of a share that is worth US$165 today. This share has experienced growth of roughly US$160 in the last 15 years.

Dividend shares are more geared towards generating an income for their shareholders. Investors generally invest in dividend shares to generate an ongoing income or cash flow. The main purpose of a dividend share is to produce a dividend, regardless of whether the share's overall value goes up or down.

For instance: the Coca-Cola Company share price is relatively volatile, jumping from around US$46 in April 2019 to around US$58 the following February and, just two months later in April 2020, dropping down to approximately US$44 again. While the share value was a rollercoaster, the share paid ongoing and pretty consistent dividends to shareholders.

Can you buy a share that delivers both growth and dividends? Absolutely! Sometimes, we get the ones like an Apple share, that has increased significantly in value over time but that has also paid very nice dividends. These are my favourite, for obvious reasons, but they're rare.

Now, out of growth and dividend shares, which is the better type of share to invest in and add to your portfolio?

I think you already know my answer to this question . . .

It depends.

It depends on what stage of life you're in, what your goals are, what your financial situation is and what you're aiming to achieve. When it comes to deciding between growth and dividend shares, one is not necessarily better than the other.

Each also carries different risks. If you're a little older, maybe you want a dividend share, because you're more focused on creating a passive income from your portfolio. Dividend shares are often a little bit more expensive than growth shares, because they're generally established businesses at a pretty tried-and-true stage of business growth.

When you buy a bank share, it's not because you're thinking, 'Sick, I think this is gonna triple over the next three years, they're on a growth run!' No, you're buying it because you recognise that it's a reliable investment in the Australian marketplace, they pay nice dividends on a regular basis and they're safe and secure. You're saying, 'Yes, I would like a steady income stream from regular dividends, thank you very much.'

But perhaps you can't afford that bank share. If you're younger and your salary income covers your day-to-day living costs and you don't need the cash flow right away, then a growth share might be more suitable. You could look for a more affordable growth share with big prospects.

I know someone who chases after dividend shares, even though she already earns a healthy six-figure income. She doesn't need the dividend on a month-to-month basis so she might be better off adding growth shares to her portfolio to increase her overall investment position.

But everyone makes their own decisions, hopefully based on their own values, goals and risk profiles, so there is no 'right' or 'wrong' answer here.

To qualify: there are 'right' and 'wrong' investing *outcomes*, and the last thing I want to happen is for you to read one sexy headline about a share that is going gangbusters and then sink your hard-earned money into that share! That can be a really easy way to lose money – fast – because you're not making an educated decision. You're making a FOMO-induced decision, and FOMO decisions are rarely good ones.

I want you to make these decisions from a place of empowerment and education. Before you begin, the most important thing is that you ask yourself questions about why you're investing, and start to think about what you actually want to achieve. Obviously, you want to make money, but why? And how? Would a dividend share that pays you $1,000 a year impact your budget and your quality of life? Or would a growing nest egg of growth shares give you more peace of mind?

What are blue chip shares?

And why do we hear so much about them?

You've probably heard of blue chip shares because Grandpa wants you to buy them and they're boring. But they're boring in a good way, like vanilla ice cream and early nights!

A blue chip share is likely to be in a big, established company. We're talking about those huge companies where you assume all the people in senior leadership wear designer suits to work every day and carry expensive briefcases and have really fancy board meetings with little sandwiches on big platters.

The reason they're blue chip shares is because they're usually large (possibly international) companies that have been operating for many years and are considered to be very stable. Such companies are generally known for having good management and they usually have a very strong financial structure, are sitting on very good cash flow and/or have a long history of solid financial performance. These shares have proven they have been able to endure previous challenging market conditions and provide investors with consistent returns in good market conditions. Because they are highly reputable and traditionally have records of stable or rising dividends, they're considered a safe harbour during an economic downturn.

Essentially, a blue chip share is a 'quality' share. (The term comes from blue chips in poker and gambling, which are high value.) Examples in Australia include Woolworths, Telstra and the Big Four banks. Blue chip shares are usually dividend shares, because they're not here to smash up the market or to grow massively. They are tried, they are true, they are steady. They are about running a functional, profitable business.

Some investors like blue chip shares based on the theory that strong financial reports of the companies mean income is protected (although not guaranteed). To contrast this, inexperienced investors often pick shares that they believe will make them rich quickly. Investors who have already acquired their own portfolio or wealth usually focus on establishing sustainable income for the future. Even if those investments offer average rates of return compared to some of the shinier, more exciting shares out there, that trade-off is considered worthwhile, as it allows those investors to protect their existing wealth and investments with stable investments.

Active versus passive investing

We've covered some of the main terms and phrases, so now you hopefully feel that you have a solid understanding of the types of shares you can buy, and what outcomes you can expect.

Next, I want to show you how all of this feeds into the concept of active versus passive investing.

Active investing is, as the name suggests, active. It's far more hands-on, and requires somebody to act in the role of the investment manager to make ongoing decisions – either you or a portfolio manager. The main goal of active investing is to get a higher return than the average of what the share market is returning.

To contrast this, we've got **passive investing**. This is a style of long-term investing. The goal of a passive investment isn't to beat the market, but to generate consistent, ongoing profits over a long period. Examples of passive investments include index funds such as exchange traded funds (ETFs) which are buying the index (more on these below), or buying the ASX top 200 to take the average of the average.

An active investing strategy might be suitable if: you have some wealth behind you already, you have a decent tolerance for risk and you want to generate strong returns that can be higher than the market average.

Adopting an active investing strategy is more expensive in terms of fees because of overheads like research and access to data. Portfolio managers are also usually quite expensive, because they've had years of experience putting together portfolios.

A passive investing strategy might be suitable if: you are happy with results that slowly grow your wealth over time, you're not in a rush to make huge profits and you have a lower risk tolerance. With a passive strategy, you can do things like buy into the top five performers, buy into the S&P 500 or the ASX top 200, and your results will ebb and flow, but over the long term they're likely to trend with the rest of the market. It's all very automated, with the mindset that you're going to buy and hold that share for a long period of time i.e. ten years or more.

By now, you probably have a pretty good idea of whether you want to be a super hands-on, deep-diving, active share investor, or if you're more aligned to the idea of handing your money over to a trusted source to invest on your behalf in a passive strategy.

What other considerations come into this, in addition to cost and risk tolerance?

- Existing knowledge of the share market.
- Time and energy to educate yourself and actually spend pursuing your investment goals.
- Desire to learn and be heavily involved versus wanting a more cruisy, hands-off approach.
- Your changing mindset and lifestyle. Your approach can and likely will change over time; you might start with a passive strategy, and then move on to active as you feel more comfortable and knowledgeable.

Direct versus indirect investing

Another thing to consider as you decide exactly what investing path to go down is whether you want to be a direct or indirect investor.

Direct investing is buying directly from the company and holding that share in your own name. The ASX sends you a little certificate (see box below) to say you are the direct owner of that actual percentage of that company. You have complete autonomy over the decisions you make related to this share and can sell, buy or trade at any time.

Indirect investing is buying shares in a company through something like an ETF, an index fund or a managed fund.

WHAT ON EARTH IS CHESS SPONSORSHIP – AND WHY SHOULD I CARE?

Okay, I'll try to make this pretty black-and-white for you (didn't you just love my little chess joke there?). CHESS sponsorship is all about direct ownership of shares. CHESS stands for Clearing House Electronic Subregister System and it's the system by which the ASX tracks who owns which shares. If your shares are CHESS-sponsored it means you own them directly, the ASX knows that and the shares are attached to you with an ID number. You hold voting rights, should also receive any dividends payable directly into your bank account, and can move your shares between platforms pretty easily.

What's the alternative, I hear you ask? Well, other platforms have a custodian model instead, whereby the custodian holds the shares on your behalf and the broker passes on dividends and decides your level of voting rights (and participation in shareholder schemes like capital raises). While you don't get direct ownership, trading costs are usually lower. This approach also allows you to access shares in fractional amounts as well as overseas shares.

What is an exchange traded fund (ETF)?

Think of an ETF as a big bucket. When you buy shares in an ETF, you're adding your money to the bucket rather than buying the shares directly. The ETF then takes the collected money and buys shares on behalf of you and all the other investors who have put their money in the same bucket.

The owner of that share is actually whoever owns the bucket, not you, so you don't have any say over when that share is bought, when that share is sold, or what action is taken. In buying into an ETF, you have effectively said, 'I trust the person who owns this bucket.'

The big benefit of an ETF is that you get instant diversification, because that ETF isn't invested in one company, but has lots of different companies in its bucket. An ETF usually has a fund manager who tracks the value of the index or asset, and when you invest in an ETF, you're relying on the smarts of somebody who's done it before and studied it and who has genuine expertise to help you put your money to work.

In terms of drawbacks, the shares aren't in your name, and transparency and control aren't high.

I really like the benefits of investments like ETFs. It's not easy to consistently and meaningfully time or beat the market, and ETFs are low-maintenance investments.

Best suits? A balanced, growth or high-growth investor who doesn't want to be too 'in the weeds' with their investment portfolio every day. ETFs allow you to adopt a passive strategy and invest in a broad selection of companies so the average person can buy the average of the market (buy a whole segment and access the average return of the market, as opposed to buying a single share), rather than beating it.

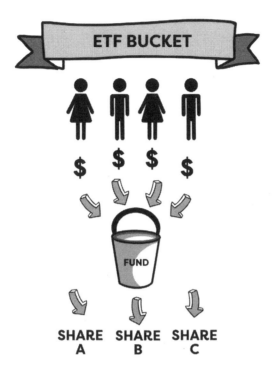

What is an index fund?

An index fund is a portfolio of shares or bonds designed to mimic the composition and performance of a financial market index.

On the plus side, the returns you get from an index fund are usually quite steady as they track the average of the top 200 companies over time, so they suit investors with a relatively low risk tolerance. The trade-off for this low risk is that the returns are, by definition, average as they track the relevant market.

For instance, you might choose an index fund that is going to mimic the ASX 200 Index Fund, which means it's going to track the average of those top 200 companies over time. There are different index funds that are designed to mimic different markets or different industries, such as a technology index fund. An index fund can even be an ETF, but the portfolio is constructed in a way that it's just tracking averages.

The most important thing to remember is that the goal of an index fund is not to outperform the market; it exists to be the average.

Bottom line? An index fund is like your trustworthy friend who will always show up and never let you down, but who won't buy you designer shoes any time soon.

This type of fund best suits a passive investor who wants something that is low cost, low energy and low maintenance with a slow-and-steady-wins-the-race approach. If you don't want to have a lot to do with your portfolio but you want to invest, an index fund could be for you.

What is a managed fund?

Managed funds work in a similar way to an ETF, where all the money is put in the bucket together. However, an ETF is listed on the stock exchange whereas a managed fund is private, making a managed fund comparatively less accessible and potentially less transparent.

Hot tip: An ETF is a type of managed fund, but not every managed fund is an ETF!

A managed fund is a professionally managed bucket, with an investment manager or a portfolio manager who goes and buys investments and manages them on your behalf.

You pay a fee for that service, but in exchange you get access to their unique smarts, and also to investment opportunities that you don't have access to as an individual investor.

For instance, you might choose to invest in a property managed fund because you can't afford to buy a property on your own, but you want exposure to that asset class. The managed fund buys and sells commercial properties, so you invest your $5,000 into the bucket and that gets pooled with all the other investors' money. Now, you're investing in a managed fund that is making decisions on millions of dollars' worth of property.

A managed fund is a 'registered managed investment scheme', which is a type of unit trust you can buy into. The number of units you buy is proportionate to the amount of money you've invested and though their value will fluctuate depending on performance, that number will stay the same unless you buy more or sell some. That managed fund might have 10,000 units and you own 200 of them. But the fund is doing well and growing, and they decide to issue more tickets, because they want more people in the fund. Suddenly, there's another 10,000 available.

There are a few advantages to investing in managed funds. You're investing with others, so buying into such a fund tends to be more affordable than buying individual shares yourself. Your and others' capital is being invested in a number of different businesses, which helps spread the risk if one or two are performing badly. And you have a professional fund manager doing the hard work, which is good if you don't have the time or experience to make informed decisions yourself.

How to begin investing in shares directly

Now, if your interest in investing has been sparked and you're ready to go deep and invest directly in shares, that's amazing too. I've written Chapter 10 of this book with people like you in mind. There are a number of ways you can get started, including DIY share trading platforms, or by engaging a financial adviser or fund manager.

If this is the path you want to go down, my suggestion is to start with micro-investing.

Micro-investing is exactly what it sounds like: investing on a really small scale, with micro amounts of capital. You can literally invest with as little as $1.

Micro-investing is all about accessibility and it truly is a ground-breaking and relatively new way to become familiar with share investing and to get used to trading with small amounts before you leverage up into bigger investments. Micro-investing allows you to have a well-diversified portfolio while you find your feet in the investment world.

Hot tip: A cool feature of some micro-investing platforms is automatic round-ups. You can set up this option in your account and when you make purchases, the figures will be rounded up to the nearest dollar and that bit extra will shoot into your investment fund. The idea is you'll barely even notice and your investments will receive lots of regular little boosts to help them grow. Check out the tables on pages 259–61 for more on investing platforms.

The robots are coming!

Robo-advice is advice that has been generated, at least in part, by an artificial intelligence algorithm. A recent Research Dive report[13] indicates that the global robo advisory market is set to grow by 39 per cent each year until 2028, so it's definitely on the rise!

There seems to be a lot of apprehension in the She's on the Money community and perhaps even the community at large about robo-advice, with fears that the advice is not quality, because it's not been generated by a human being.

Some believe that it's automated, therefore it can't be that personal.

My take? I genuinely believe that a chunk of my job as a financial adviser in ten years is going to be replaced by robo-advice. And I'm actually perfectly okay with that!

Why? Because crunching the numbers and generating the actual investment options is the least meaningful part of my job. That's the part of the job that a robo-adviser can quite adequately take over.

But there's a really important part of my job that cannot be replaced: my ability to manage a relationship, to support my clients through life events, and to help them understand their options and make decisions. We all crave human interaction, at the end of the day. A robot can't really factor in the mindset and emotional issues, and ask the client: how do you feel about that? In this way, I simply don't believe robo-advice can replace truly personal advice.

So, I think my value as an adviser in the years to come is increasingly going to be around relationship management, helping my clients achieve their goals and live the lives that they want to live, because of the expertise I can offer and the value I can add to their journey. While investment is well suited to automation, things like insurance and superannuation absolutely require a human touch. I'm going to have less and less to do with the investment side of my business, not because I necessarily want to, but because the robots are smarter than I am. The plus side is that it will free up more of my time, energy and focus for assisting my clients in creating their best lives!

A NOTE ON TAX AND YOUR SHARE INVESTMENTS

It's important to be aware from the get-go that if you make money out of your share investments, the Australian Taxation Office (ATO) is going to want to know about it so they can take their clip of the ticket.

Later in this book I dedicate an entire chapter to tax, but here's a quick summary when it comes to tax and share investing.

The type of tax you pay depends on the type of share you invest in, how profit is generated, and when you buy and sell.

As an investor, capital gains tax (CGT) may be payable on your shares when you sell them, or when another CGT event happens, such as if you:

- accept an offer from a company to buy back your shares;
- receive a distribution from a unit trust or managed fund (other than a dividend);
- receive non-assessable payments from a company;
- own shares in a company that is taken over by or merges with another company;
- redeem units in a managed fund by switching from one fund to another; or
- make an *in specie* transfer, also known as an off-market transfer, where assets are transferred in and out of super funds without the need to convert them into cash.

CGT is not charged on dividends you receive from your investments – these are taxed as ordinary income, so the amount of tax you pay will depend on your individual income tax bracket. You may be entitled to franking credits, if the company has already paid tax.

One last thing: remember to consult your accountant or tax adviser (if you have one) to cover everything off properly.

● ● ● ● ● ●

LAURA, 29 – ACT

I love investing in shares. The first time I received a dividend was so exciting, even though it was only $1.70. Seeing my hard-earned money create a passive income made financial freedom seem possible. When the market drops it can be disheartening at first, but then I started to see the dips as a sale. I was able to purchase more shares for the same amount of money, which should help grow my portfolio in the future.

TISHENA, 30 – NSW

I started investing in shares over the last nine months. I put it off for a long time, not knowing how to get into the market and being scared (risk-averse). My experience started with listening to She's on the Money . . . a lot! Then freaking out that I'm not where I should be or could be and that I needed to pull my finger out. I spoke to a financial adviser to help me and got to a strategy I was comfortable with and could execute myself. When I decided to take the plunge, at first I was terrified. As I went along drip-feeding my house deposit into the market, I got more confident and tried my hand at watching some individual shares versus ETFs. I made a bit of an oopsies but thankfully not one that will cost me greatly. Watching the market fall was uncomfortable, but constant reminders that it's not a loss unless it's crystallised helps a lot. Plus my goal is dividends!

SAMANTHA, 29 – QLD

I have an auto-transfer to my investing account each pay and when I reach $1,000, I buy more shares. I'm also on a dividend reinvestment plan. I used to check my stocks every day and now I have a bit of a look every few months to see how it's going. I have to keep telling myself this is a long-term investment so there is no point worrying about the day-to-day fluctuations in the market. I was a bit scared to invest but after about a year using micro-investing platforms, I felt I'd reached a point where I could take that next step. So far, I'm happy with how I'm going and proud to be the first person in my family who invests.

● ● ● ● ● ●

TAKE NOTE

Getting across the different types of shares that exist will help you make the most informed decision before you dive in.

....

I suggest working out whether growth or dividends are more important to you, and whether you'd prefer a more active or passive approach to share investing if you want to pursue it.

....

Understanding the difference between micro-investing, share trading platforms and robo-advice is crucial – all are different and service different needs.

....

Chapter 7

A deep dive into property

Many people find the concept of property investing a little more familiar than share trading or other investment classes because real estate is already part of their everyday life. We live in homes. We rent them, we buy them, we upsize and downsize as our needs and lifestyles change. And throughout this process, we can make some money. Big money. *Huge* money.

If you've been fortunate enough to own property through a growth spurt, or someone close to you has, then you know there's the potential to enjoy great returns in the property market. But it's also possible to lose money, if you buy a poor performing property asset, or you buy and sell at the wrong time in the cycle.

As much as I would like to, it would be impossible to give you a comprehensive guide to buying an investment property in just one chapter (it would be a *veeery* long chapter!). It's also a really personal experience.

This chapter is here to help you understand property as an asset class, and to challenge your own thoughts, values and beliefs on what property as an investment might look like for you.

Preconceptions and privilege

First up, it's important to understand that investing in property is really different to buying real estate to live in.

Yes, technically your family home *is* an asset – it's made of bricks and mortar and it's going to grow in value and decline in value and then grow again, and it's going to do all of the things that assets tend to do. But I tell my clients not to consider their family home as an investment because you don't purchase it with the pure intention of making a profit. That's rarely the driver behind decisions around your own home – the driver is instead often emotional, or the necessity of having a roof over your head. For me, it was security and having the creativity to do whatever I wanted inside my own four walls.

Furthermore, you don't want your own home to be an asset that you are forced to consider selling if your financial position suddenly changes. No one wants to have to sell their home because it's their only real way out of a financial pickle. A family home is there to put a roof over your head. You don't want to be forced into liquidating that asset and downsizing. That's why owning a home that you live in serves a very different purpose to owning a property that you intend to produce a profit out of.

Second, I want to acknowledge that I come from a very privileged position when I talk about property. Why? Because I'm a property owner.

When my partner and I started looking at property, the average home price in Melbourne was around ten times my annual salary. That was a massive shock to the system. Still, I was able to buy my home and I recognise that puts me in a position of privilege when we're having this conversation.

Back when my dad was a first home buyer at the ripe age of 21, the average home price was around three times the average annual income, and most people had the reasonable expectation that they could buy their first home in their twenties. That's just the way it was back then! You grew up, you started working, you bought a property and you made a home. Property wasn't just for the rich; it was even for the mum and dad who worked at the local milk bar. Most people were able to earn an income that would support them getting a bank loan and buying their first house.

I look at the young people around me – smart, savvy, successful people earning really good salaries – and they're all struggling to get into the property market. They have been saving for a really long time. They're earning six figures yet they're still finding it super tough to get in the market.

That sentence sounds ridiculous! To be earning six figures and you can't get into the property market? *That shouldn't be a thing!* It's also really frustrating. But it highlights the fact that the reality of the home-buying process has changed. It's simply not as easy as it once was.

Average capital city property prices are now more than 11 times the average disposable income – back in the early 1990s, prices were less than six times the average disposable income. Surprise surprise, the numbers are especially jaw-dropping in the two biggest capitals: in Melbourne, house prices exceed average local incomes by 18 times and in Sydney it's a staggering 23 times! And while it might seem simple to assume that this is a result of interest rates, the truth of the matter is that houses are less and less affordable and income growth just is not keeping up with property prices.

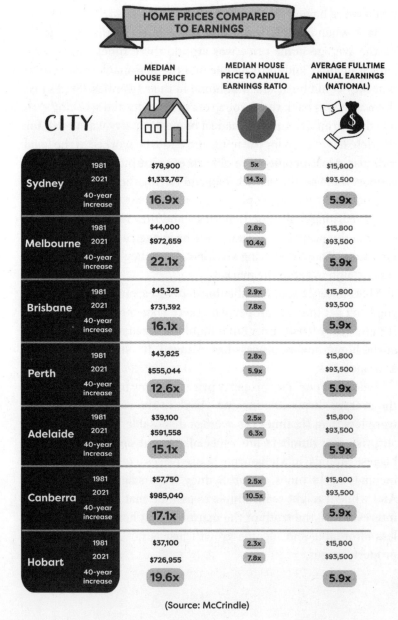

HOME PRICES COMPARED TO EARNINGS

CITY		MEDIAN HOUSE PRICE	MEDIAN HOUSE PRICE TO ANNUAL EARNINGS RATIO	AVERAGE FULLTIME ANNUAL EARNINGS (NATIONAL)
Sydney	1981	$78,900	5x	$15,800
	2021	$1,333,767	14.3x	$93,500
	40-year increase	**16.9x**		**5.9x**
Melbourne	1981	$44,000	2.8x	$15,800
	2021	$972,659	10.4x	$93,500
	40-year increase	**22.1x**		**5.9x**
Brisbane	1981	$45,325	2.9x	$15,800
	2021	$731,392	7.8x	$93,500
	40-year increase	**16.1x**		**5.9x**
Perth	1981	$43,825	2.8x	$15,800
	2021	$555,044	5.9x	$93,500
	40-year increase	**12.6x**		**5.9x**
Adelaide	1981	$39,100	2.5x	$15,800
	2021	$591,558	6.3x	$93,500
	40-year increase	**15.1x**		**5.9x**
Canberra	1981	$57,750	2.5x	$15,800
	2021	$985,040	10.5x	$93,500
	40-year increase	**17.1x**		**5.9x**
Hobart	1981	$37,100	2.3x	$15,800
	2021	$726,955	7.8x	$93,500
	40-year increase	**19.6x**		**5.9x**

(Source: McCrindle)

In my experience, property has psychologically been tied closely to safety for Australians – particularly older generations, who pass down that concept of the 'Australian dream' of home owner-ship. That plays a lot into the modern mindset about property, even though its accessibility is now completely different to what it used to be.

What hasn't changed, however, is our cultural obsession with owning real estate. Australians *love* property. We're completely head over heels for it. We dedicate countless hours to TV shows showing us how to buy, sell and renovate, and once we own prop-erty, we become obsessed with the options available to spruce it up.

Interestingly, owning property doesn't necessarily mean financial security anymore. In fact, it could actually mean the opposite, if you're forcing yourself to save for a property that you can't afford. Or worse, if you own a property and you're living pay cheque to pay cheque, doing maintenance and repairs has the potential to send you broke.

I thought about this just recently, because my air-conditioning system broke. It's a reverse-cycle ducted air-con system which goes through the entire house, and it's completely cactus. We were quoted $12,500 to replace it. *Fantastic.*

We have an emergency fund, and we're so very fortunate that this unexpected cost is not going to financially cripple us, but it's still a huge amount of money I'd absolutely rather not have to spend.

This is why you have to be *really* ready for everything that owning property entails. It's not just about saving the deposit and qualifying for the loan; it's also about all of the ongoing costs and responsibilities.

So before you go too far down the path of wanting to invest in this way, I first encourage you to consider: do you really *want* to own a property? Or are you culturally wired to *think* it's what you want?

Purchasing property as an investment

Let's turn our attention to property as an investment class. Do I think property is a good investment? Yes, it can be. Do I think it is suitable and accessible to everyone? No, I don't.

And do I think that the cultural importance we place on owning property puts too much pressure on millennials and younger Australians to live 'the way that we used to live' when the world around us has completely changed? Yes, I do.

And finally, is it fair to put that pressure on the next generation? Absolutely not!

I don't think you need to own a property to be financially successful, but that's just my personal view. Your own take on this will boil down to your values and what you want to achieve in your lifetime. Your views and decisions when it comes to property will be unique to your own circumstances.

If you want to invest in property, you need to budget for the following:

The deposit: usually between 10 and 20 per cent of the purchase price. On a $500,000 purchase price, you'd need $50,000 to $100,000 as a deposit.

Stamp duty: this is a levy charged by the state government. Its total, usually a percentage of the purchase price, depends on your state or territory as well as your personal circumstances.

Lender's mortgage insurance: a one-off insurance premium your bank usually requires you to take out if your deposit is worth less than 20 per cent of the purchase price. It protects the bank if you default on your loan, but they require you to pay for the policy as a condition of giving you the loan. You can usually add this to the loan rather than paying it upfront, but that means you'll pay interest on it over time. LMI premiums are usually several thousand dollars, and can even be as high as $20,000 or more.

Other buying costs: like legal fees, inspections and bank fees. You can budget to spend around $5,000 on these buying costs, give or take.

Overall, the cost of buying a property is really not cheap and a lot of the costs are upfront. But many people have made a lot of money out of property over time, and here's how.

When you invest in property, you can make money in two ways: capital growth and yield.

Growth is when the value of the property goes up. A house that you buy for $500,000 today might be worth $1 million in ten years, so you benefit from that capital growth. You have to sell the property to unlock that value, a process that comes with its own challenges and costs.

Yield is the rent you receive on a weekly, fortnightly or monthly basis from the tenants your property is leased to.

When you own an investment property, you need to pay for a number of things, including the interest rate, mortgage repayment, council rates, strata fees, property management fees, repairs and insurance. If the rent you receive covers all of this and more, the extra money you make is your profit. In this case your property would be defined as being positively geared.

Hot tip: You can calculate a property's yield by multiplying the weekly rent (e.g. $500) × 52 weeks (e.g. $26,000) × 100 (e.g. $2,600,000) then divide it by the property value (e.g. $500,000). You can compare yields for different areas and property types (such as units or houses) to help assess their relative performance as investments. It's also important as a way to understand whether the property would put you ahead in terms of your cash flow.

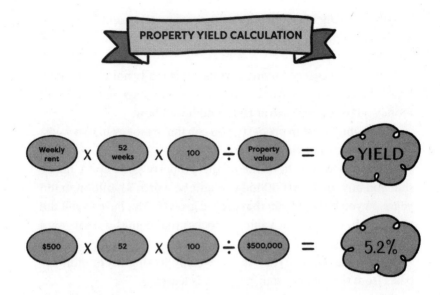

In this example, the yield is 5.2 per cent. If the interest you're paying on your mortgage is 2.5 per cent and the yield is 5.2 per cent then, in simple terms, the maths shows us that you're making a profit each week because the yield is higher. This really basic calculation doesn't factor in other costs of owning the property, though. When interest rates are higher, the opposite is true: if you were paying 5.5 per cent for your mortgage and the yield is 5.2 per cent, you're losing money on the investment each week.

So, why would anyone intentionally invest in an asset, knowing that if the rent doesn't cover the mortgage and other maintenance costs then it'll cost them money, week after week?

Property investors do this with a goal of experiencing strong capital growth.

Capital growth comes in a couple of ways. One way is through manufacturing growth. For instance, if you renovate to improve the aesthetic and function of the property, that can increase its value.

The other way to experience capital growth is through market changes. When the property market is going through a 'boom' phase, property prices go up. We saw this recently in 2021, when Australian property markets (generally speaking, each state and territory is slightly different, and suburbs and areas within each city or regional location have different growth drivers) grew in value by an average of 22 per cent.[14] Sydney and Melbourne also experienced booms from 2015–2017.

Remember, though, that this growth is not a linear, solid line, forever going up. Property prices fluctuate. Over the last 25 years, for instance, Sydney's average capital growth for houses each year was 7.6 per cent, reports CoreLogic.[15] But that's the average – not the whole story. If we zoom in a little on that line, as in this graph of annual change from across the past 20 years, we get a picture of many ups and downs:

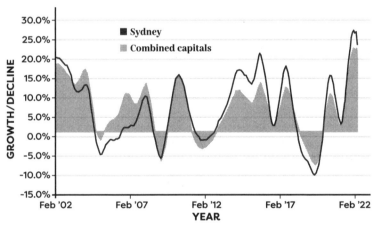

Sydney annual change in property prices
(Source: CoreLogic)

The most successful property investors are those who hold for a long time, so they can weather the 'drops' in the market and take advantage of the 'peaks'. A bit like with the share market, it's about staying in the property market for a long time and waiting for it to gradually increase, rather than reacting when there are dips or spikes.

But, as this graph shows, it's easy to lose money in property. Imagine if you bought at the peak of the market then sold at the trough: you'd lose potentially hundreds of thousands of dollars.

This is a very possible outcome when it comes to property because you need a loan (a mortgage) to invest. If that loan becomes too expensive for you to manage, either because interest rates have increased or the rental income has been impacted, you could be in a position where you're forced to sell.

This is where people can run into serious financial trouble, which is why it's essential that you consider all of the risks before diving into a property investment.

That said, when you look at this data, you can see that property can be a financially rewarding asset class over the long term. If you buy a quality property when you're 25 and hold it until you're 65, you get the benefit of 40 years in the market and there's potential to make a significant amount of profit.

I think this is a good time to issue a qualifier, for the sake of utmost clarity: I'm an experienced financial planner, and I've helped hundreds of my clients to structure their portfolios with property assets inside them. But I am not a property expert.

I'm not suggesting that one type of property or investing strategy is better or worse, because the reality is, property investing is a very personalised experience. The right advice for you is likely to be *really* different to the right advice for your sister, your best friend or your next-door neighbour.

For instance, you could invest in a residential home. Or you could look into commercial real estate – things like offices, retail space, warehouses, factories and more. They may not seem as sexy or as accessible as buying residential properties, but if the aim of the game is solely making money, then these types of investments can drive a strong return.

This is partly because with a commercial investment, the tenant can pay for way more than a standard housing tenant does. Everything from council rates and strata fees often are their financial responsibility, not yours. Yields on commercial invest-ments can therefore stretch up to 7 per cent, 8 per cent, 10 per cent or even higher.

Commercial properties are (typically, but not always) a little more expensive than residential properties, and you usually need a bigger deposit of around 20–40 per cent in order to get a loan. You can also experience longer vacancies with a commercial tenant, so you need to have the funds behind you to pay for the costs of owning the property during any periods when no rent is coming in.

Now, in your personal situation, a commercial investment might not make sense. The deposit is too big, the vacancy risks too high and the overall proposition is unsuitable. But your next-door neighbour? The one with a big inheritance sitting in her bank, who wants to invest in an asset that generates a high yield each year so she can cut back to part-time hours? For her, a commercial property could be just the investment she's looking for.

As with any asset class, investing in property is personal. And complex.

Is property actually a good investment?

As we've seen, you can win or lose with property. Just the same way as you can win or lose in the share market. Every investment has its risks.

Before jumping head first into property, there are a few things that are important to note. Firstly, there's a common phrase, 'safe as houses', the implication being that investing in property is always a fairly safe bet. I'd argue that's not the case. Secondly, you need to consider diversification. Heard the phrase 'don't put all your eggs in one basket'? If you were to choose property as your main and only investment, this is what you'd be doing. I'm not saying don't do that, but I am saying just be aware of concen-trating lots of risk in one asset.

Here are some of the key pros and cons of property investing:

✓ **It's real and tangible.** Property is bricks and mortar and tiles and carpet. You can drive past it, visit it on weekends and even plan to live in it if your financial world goes topsy-turvy and that becomes necessary.

✓ **A tenant helps you pay off your asset.** The cost of owning an investment property can be contributed to by the rent your tenant pays. If the rent covers the interest, repayment of principal and any other costs associated with the property, over time the income from your tenants could help you eventually own the asset outright, in full, while reducing how much you have to dip into money from your other income sources to pay it off.

✓ **You can leverage your money.** When you invest in property, you'll often get a mortgage. This allows you to take a smaller pool of funds – say $50,000 – and use it to leverage into a $500,000 investment, which increases your potential gain (and your potential risk).

✓ **There can be significant tax benefits.** I'll go into these more in Chapter 12 but a few main pluses to note here. First, if your property is negatively geared – meaning the income from rent doesn't cover the ongoing deductible costs of owning the asset – then the gap between the two figures (income and cost) can generally be claimed on your tax return. Second, if you've owned the property for at least twelve months and you sell it, you should be eligible for a 50 per cent capital gains discount. Third, you may be able to claim a tax deduction for other related expenses such as land tax, water charges, council rates, pest control, cleaning, repairs and maintenance, insurance, advertising fees to find a new tenant and more. (Refer to the ATO website for the most up-to-date information.)

✓ **It's possible to negotiate.** When you invest in shares and bonds, the price you pay is set by the market. When you invest in property, a huge range of variables can impact how much you pay and, as a result, it's possible to negotiate the price.

✓ **You have ongoing expert help.** Most property investors work with a property manager to help them take care of their property day-to-day, which means you have an expert on your team who can, ideally, help you maximise your income and minimise your pain – both financial and time.

✗ **It's (often prohibitively) expensive.** You'll need tens of thousands of dollars for the deposit, perhaps even six figures. Then you'll need to take out a huge loan from the bank. In addition to the capital you need to start (the deposit), you also have to secure a mortgage.

✗ **Buying and selling costs are also huge.** You'll pay stamp duty, legal and bank fees on the way in. And then you'll pay whopping agents' commission, possibly some capital gains tax and even more legal fees on the way out. These can account for tens of thousands of dollars – gone.

✗ **It's not 'set-and-forget'.** Owning an investment property can be a really time-consuming exercise, even if you have a great property manager. There are the ongoing maintenance and repairs, along with replacing things when they break, and the work that comes with balancing the books and managing the paperwork. Expect to dedicate some time.

✗ **Property isn't a liquid asset.** When you invest in property, you're essentially locking your money up. If you really need it in a flash, property is one of the hardest assets to extract said cash from, because you'll need to either sell or refinance – both of which takes weeks, if not months.

✗ **Property management can be painful.** Not all property managers are created equal. A great one will help you minimise stress and take care of daily hassles for you, but an inexperienced or overworked manager can make your property journey even more exhausting and time-consuming than it needs to be.

Bottom line: investing in property requires more time and energy than other forms of investing.

Yes, I want to get into the property market

Let's say you work out that this kind of investment is aligned to your values and goals. That's great for you! Assuming that you find that your budget doesn't quite give you the choices you were hoping for, you have a few options:

Rentvest. This is where you invest in a more affordable property and become a landlord, while you continue to rent in the areas where you'd prefer to live. When you rentvest, you could buy a property in a completely different suburb, city or even state. It's another way to step up (see below).

Delay. You've identified that you want to buy a property, but right now your budget doesn't quite allow you to achieve that goal. You might have to turn it into a longer-term goal while you keep saving and growing your wealth, with a plan to buy once your income supports it.

Step up. This is the traditional stepping stone that generations of the past used again and again (albeit during much more affordable times). You start with a small one-bedroom apartment or a tiny house in the outer suburbs and step it up from there, selling the current home and buying a bigger one as the market grows, your income grows, and you can afford to upgrade.

These are not the only ways to get into the property market, of course. There are literally dozens of different things you could do: buy in a syndicate or a group, or buy with a friend or sibling. Co-purchase a property with your parents, or have them come on board as guarantors.

This is where I want to issue a bit of a warning: I don't necessarily advocate for these strategies, as I've seen too many of them fail. But your story is your own to plot out and learn for yourself as you go, so I'm not going to tell you not to go down that path.

What I will say is this:

- Whatever strategy you use to get into the property market, engage good lawyers and get *everything* in writing.
- Don't let FOMO push you into the property market sooner than you're actually ready. It's expensive to be a home owner.

And lastly, remember:

- Don't think of your family home as an asset.

A note on rentvesting

So, you've decided you want to be a property owner and that you want to buy a property as an investor. If this is the case, then the things that you look for are very different to what you look at when you want to own the property to live in.

This is because things that are important to you personally – like a kitchen with loads of bench space, a big linen closet to store all your fluffy towels, a bedroom with a built-in closet, or an apartment complex where everyone has their own personal laundry – might not be as important to a tenant.

You'll pay more for a property that has more features and amenities and bells and whistles, but will that translate to a better return on investment? You may also consider what tenants in your area or price bracket will expect, and what they will pay more for.

I also want you to be aware that certain financial support packages out there don't apply to property purchases if you're not going to live there, at least for a specified period of time, such as some of those for first-time buyers. So do your research on the terms and conditions of financial support you might intend to apply for with an investment property purchase.

There's something for everybody but not everything is for everybody, so while rentvesting can be a fabulous option for some people, don't worry if for whatever reason it doesn't suit you!

BUYING WITH A FRIEND

You might think it's a good idea to buy a property with your brother or cousin or friend because two incomes are better than one, and you can both get into the property market sooner. And you think that makes a lot of sense.

But when you go down this path, you suddenly become dependent on and entangled with somebody else's financial situation. What if you and a co-buyer invest in a property, then three years later, your co-buyer is in a relationship and they tell you they want to sell to buy something with their partner?

What if it turns out the person you've bought a property with has a totally different value set than you do? What if that person loses their job and stops paying for their share of the bills associated with the property?

It's a little different when planning to buy with a partner. In that situation, the whole plan stems from being on the same financial trajectory. You're not trying to do life separately then coming together for this one purchase; you're doing life together, and the purpose of buying the investment property is to build wealth together.

That said, tying your financial wellness and future financial health up with somebody else can be a really big risk, even if you adore them right now. It might not always be that way – and you could end up in a world of pain (financially and emotionally) if it all goes pear-shaped.

● ● ● ● ● ●

JESS, 29 – NT

I was very fortunate to buy my own home in May 2020, just prior to the COVID property boom. I then moved in with my partner 12 months later and sold my property, making a 50 per cent return, which I've now put into shares. It wasn't without its downsides, including major water leaks and body corporate issues – hence the decision to sell.

MARY, 35 – QLD

I've recently put my property up for rent as I needed to move for work and it seems to be positively geared, which means it costs me less than I make from it each month. The income generated from it covers the mortgage, rates and body corp fees. But it was my first home so I did feel some emotional attachment to the thought of letting it rent to somebody else!

CONNIE, 39 – NSW

Investing from a young age and on my own in the property market allowed me the financial independence to make a decision to leave my successful, corporate role in 2018 when I essentially burnt out. I started owning property at 24 (I'm currently 39) and my experience has been mixed – some good, some bad, some ugly! Now, we own our simple, three-bedroom renovated home outright, and last year bought a rural, lifestyle block of land that we hope to build another home on down the track. But in hindsight I wish I'd had the assistance of a mentor or someone knowledgeable about the process when I started. I made a lot of rookie mistakes through lack of experience.

● ● ● ● ● ●

TAKE NOTE

When considering home ownership for living or
investing, think carefully about whether this aligns
with your values and your long-term goals.

....

Don't think of any property that you own and live in as an asset.

....

Property investments make money in two
ways: capital growth and yield.

....

Chapter 8

Ethical and ESG investing

I find this topic *fascinating*, because the meaning of 'ethical investing' is infuriatingly vague, as it represents something different for everyone. But I love the uniqueness that every individual brings to their personal finances!

This segment of the investment market can be a bit like the Wild West, because there's no official definition of what ethical investing is, or what is 'right' or 'wrong' from an ethical perspective.

In investment terms, ethical investing is essentially the practice of investing in assets and companies based on your moral or ethical principles. There are 100 shades of grey involved here, because what one person or brand or company deems to be 'ethical' might not be ethical to another.

So, where's the line?

Companies put a *lot* of time, effort and money into projecting a certain image – one that shows them in a certain light. The picture they paint, however, isn't always accurate. So this can become a slightly tricky space for the average investor to navigate.

It's just like when you go to the supermarket and you buy a bottle of liquid soap. It's called something like Great Decision Botanical Organic Care Soap. The packaging is brown and green and covered in flowers and trees, and when you add the bottle to your trolley, it feels like a good, ethical choice. It feels like you've supported a business that is making the world a better place.

In reality? It may just be greenwashing.

The soap might not be organic, nor eco-friendly. It could be plain old bog-standard chemicals wrapped up to look like something it's not, packaged and dressed up as an 'ethical' product, for which its manufacturer may have charged a premium. You just fell for some slick marketing . . .

And the same thing can happen with investing.

But never fear! I'm here to help you work out a) exactly what ethical investing means to *you*, and b) how to find companies that align with your values.

What is ethical investing to you?

There are a number of upsides of ethical investing, including sustainable returns, the potential to de-risk your portfolio, and also to live in alignment with your values. If you are putting your hard-earned money into certain companies, I'm guessing you want them to be companies making a positive contribution and not playing a part in – and profiting from – the problematic issues that exist in our world.

But as you're probably picking up by now, it's not as simple as sticking a label on something and proclaiming, 'This is ethical and good.'

To go back to our supermarket example, there are some parts

of the grocery shopping experience where it is relatively straight-forward to spot a genuinely organic product.

If you're wandering through the fruit section and you pick up an apple and there's a little organic sticker on it, you can be fairly certain that you're holding an organically certified piece of produce. The producer of that apple has paid to have its products certified to confirm that production has met the ethical standard, code or criteria for being organic here in Australia. That might mean that absolutely no pesticides have been used, or it's been produced or stored in a certain way, or grown under certain conditions. We can find that guarantee because organic is a term here in Australia that is mandated.

But ethical? That's a whole different ballgame. What is considered ethical to one company might be wildly unethical to another. It's very subjective. And that makes it all the more fun to navigate (insert sarcasm font here . . .)!

Let's break it down a bit. Overall, in the investing space, there are a few different ways ethical manifests:

- **Sustainable investing**, which balances traditional investing with environmental, social, and governance-related (ESG) insights to improve long-term outcomes.
- **Socially responsible investing**, which encourages you to consider social factors that are important to you when deciding where and how to invest your money.
- **Green/eco-investing**, which focuses on companies or projects that are committed to the conservation of natural resources.

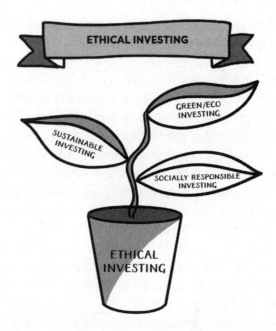

All of these actually mean different things to different companies, and sustainable, socially responsible and green investments aren't all the same things. They often get lumped into the same bucket, as if they're heading in the same direction, but in fact they're quite distinct.

Definitions of ethics vary as much for individuals as they do for companies. In my line of work, I'm lucky to meet people from all walks of life and one thing I've learned is that everyone has a different viewpoint.

You can have three people in a room who describe themselves as 'ethical' and

- one is a lifelong vegan who doesn't believe in doing anything that harms the earth or any living creature in it;
- one genuinely believes that landlords are capitalist pigs, that investing in property is for those who want to take advantage of the world; and

- one has invested in low-priced, entry-level homes that they exclusively rent to single parents, with a goal of helping to keep housing affordable for vulnerable parts of the community.

These three individuals are very different, and each has their own code of ethics, but they have very different views as to what is ethical. And in my view, that's okay!

While there are some fairly universal ethical standards, ultimately you have to create your own personal code of ethics. As with so many of the best things in financial planning, it's all about tailoring your investment choices to you.

Ethics versus ESG investing

You may have heard about environmental, social and governance (ESG) criteria. They are a set of standards for evaluating a company's operations. Ethical investing and ESG investing are in the same family, but they're not quite the same thing.

In simple terms, ESG means you're investing in companies that are rallying for change and rallying for good. When you make a decision to invest in one of these companies, it's a decision to influence positive change, and to make our world a better place by being a better investor.

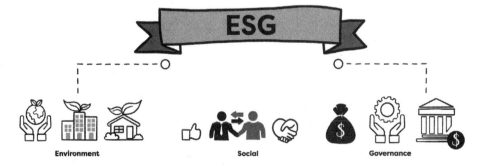

When you're looking at a company and assessing whether it's an ESG company, you're looking at its impact on the environment and its approach to sustainability, the ethics of how it runs its operation, and how its leadership sets the foundation to achieve all of the above. If it is an ESG company, it's likely it will say so in its marketing and content.

You could also look for B Corp certification. B Corps are businesses that are certified by the organisation B Lab (or one of its international affiliates) after having been deemed to meet very high standards of public transparency, social and environmental performance, and legal accountability. The assessment is rigorous and they must balance profit with purpose and be accountable to all stakeholders, not just their shareholders. B Corps are therefore likely to be strong ESG performers.

Here are some questions to ask of companies in which you're thinking of ethically investing:

● ●

ENVIRONMENT

- Do they carbon offset?
- Does their product or service create pollution?
- Do they use renewable energy sources?
- How efficient and eco-friendly is their supply chain?
- Do they use compostable packaging?
- Do they minimise packaging?
- What are their recycling and reuse practices?

SOCIAL

- Do they pay their people fairly?
- Are they outsourcing roles to staff overseas?
- Do they exploit their employees with long hours and poor pay?
- Do their people earn a liveable wage?

- How does their product or service impact the broader community?
- Is their workforce inclusive of different genders, ages and backgrounds?
- Do they drive diversity?
- Do they embrace the LGBTQIA+ community?
- Are they catering towards disability?
- Do they embrace diversity in their workforce?
- How many people in their workforce are women?
- What are their policies around harassment and bullying?
- Are they active against modern slavery?

GOVERNANCE

- Do they persist with poor corporate governance practices?
- Does the business operate with a clear code of ethics?
- Are they clear on their values?
- Is there transparency in reporting?
- Is there diversity and inclusion in their leadership?
- How many people on their board are women?

● ●

ESG is the way of the future, and it's certainly what consumers are demanding. A 2021 PWC report[16] found that 83 per cent of consumers think companies should be actively shaping ESG best practices, while almost three-quarters (74 per cent) said companies care much more about the environment than they did ten years ago.

So I feel optimistic about all of this! I genuinely believe that we are all heading towards a place where we will expect ethical companies and ESG companies to be the norm. Imagine how great that would be.

'But Victoria, what should I be focusing on: ethics or ESG?'

It's important to separate ESG from ethics and know the difference between the two when you're deciding how to invest. One way I suggest people look at it is that ESG is a socially responsible way of investing while creating a better future for ourselves, specifically through the prisms of environment, social and governance.

Ethical investing is overlaying this with your own personal values and beliefs, where your personal ethics should inform your investment strategy.

Ethical investing is about putting your money towards what you believe in, and funding things that you want to grow.

And the best part? It can result in massive profits, too. Let me tell you more about that!

Making bank from green investments

A question I hear a lot is: if I choose to invest ethically, am I giving up on the performance? Does it mean I am going to be sacrificing something?

I genuinely love this question, because I get to break the good news! The answer is no, you don't have to accept lower returns as a trade-off. That's not how it works.

Ethical investing is big business. In 2020, total assets overseen by ethical investment funds on behalf of Australian investors rose to $1.28 trillion, accounting for 40 cents of every professionally managed dollar.

According to a private accreditor of ethical investments, Responsible Investment Association Australasia (RIAA), on a global basis, the average ethical investment fund outperformed its Equity World Large Blend benchmark (funds that primarily invest in large global companies) on a one-, three- and five-year basis.[17]

Furthermore, in 2020, there was an analysis done by the Morgan Stanley Institute on sustainable investing. They looked at 3,000 US mutual funds and ETFs, and found that sustainable equity funds outperformed traditional peer funds by a median total return of 4.3 percentage points in 2020.[18]

During the same period, US sustainable bond funds beat their non-ESG counterparts by a median total return of 0.9 percentage points.

And according to Bloomberg, in the first half of 2022, Europe-focused, US-focused and global ESG equity funds did better on average than their non-ESG counterparts, losing less than the broader market.[19]

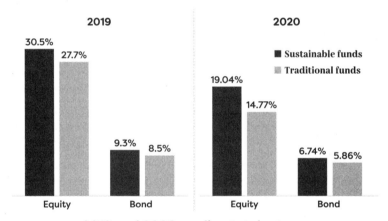

2019 and 2020 median total returns
(Source: Morgan Stanley)

So, any thought you have that by trying to chase your own values in your investment journey, you'd be compromising something? It's actually not the case. I count that as a win.

However, I should be clear, that doesn't mean it's all sunshine and roses. Some companies can become complacent when it comes to ESG compliance. They slap the label on without keeping up with the commitments that come with being an ESG company. They might have been very enthusiastic to get the initial IPO out the gate, but then the shine fades as they pay less attention to the way they're managing themselves, or they start drifting into investing in projects that aren't aligned to their core values.

What's more, as with any investment strategy, there are risks that come with ethical investing. When you take this approach, you can limit your pool of investment options, and not all ethical funds have the same potential or performance. You might also pay more in fees, partly because a lot more time, energy and effort goes into reviewing ethical funds since additional research is needed.

It's important to note that our values change over time too, as we get more educated, as our lifestyles change, as we get exposed to more people and places and facets of life. All of these things can lead to us changing our minds.

We all know someone who has become a vegan after eating meat for decades (that's me, hiya!). We've heard about that person who was previously on the picket line protesting climate change, but who churns through fast fashion with new packages arriving every other week, and thinks nothing of the carbon carnage it's causing.

We are consistently learning and changing and evolving. Eighty years ago, we didn't know smoking was bad for us. Well, some of us knew . . . but you get my point. As we change, and as our values evolve, so too will our investment decisions. It's a natural part of the process and keeps us on a path that reflects who we are.

Another important thing I want to acknowledge here is that if you decide to go down the ESG route, you are limiting your investment options. I think that can be a good thing, too. Coco Chanel famously said that you should remove one accessory before you leave the house because 'less is more'. Well, when it comes to investing, fewer options can be empowering. While you do have a smaller pool of options in the marketplace to choose from, it doesn't mean you can't still have a really well-diversified investment portfolio.

I remember sitting down with a client after a very specific phone consultation. She said she was absolutely and unequivocally an ethical investor. 'Don't worry,' I said. 'We'll tailor your plan to make sure it works for you and aligns with your goals.'

When she was sitting in front of me and I asked her specifically what an ethical investment strategy meant to her, she looked me in the eyes and said, 'I just don't want any nukes. I don't want to fund any nuclear weapons.'

Tobacco farms? Fine. Pollution-heavy coal-powered energy? Not a problem. Oil? Let's do it! She didn't care about anything other than ensuring she didn't support nuclear technology. That's what ethical investing meant to her.

I have other clients who have deeply personal reasoning behind their self-imposed ethical obligations. I had one client whose dad had a gambling problem that had caused total chaos for their family, so he was adamant that he didn't want to support gambling companies. Others will say they have issues in their family with alcohol and drug addiction, so they don't want to support tobacco and alcohol industries.

When I'm trying to help a client structure their portfolio in a way that truly aligns with their values, I might ask questions like:

- How much do you care about the Great Barrier Reef?
- What are your feelings about fossil fuels and mining?
- Do you have any issues investing in tobacco farms?
- What about dairy farms?
- Do you have religious beliefs that could impact your investment choices?

Ethical investing and superannuation

When it comes to super, there's a whole heap of options out there that are described as 'ethical' super funds. At the time of writing, four funds have been certified by the RIAA as being ethical on a whole-of-fund basis. If you want to look them up, you can find them through RIAA's Responsible Returns tool, which I'll tell you a bit more about later in the chapter. (That's not to say those are the only ethical funds available, though, and the market is evolving.)

Warning: approach fund-wide returns figures for super funds with a bit of caution and have a keen eye on the detail. Why? Because the performance of the specific option that *your* super is invested in may actually be quite different from that of the fund as a whole. The fund-wide performance figure might get a nice boost from a high-performing option within it, but your super needs to be invested in that particular option if you're going to be likely to see the benefit of its performance.

We'll come back to super again in Chapter 9.

What if you (accidentally) invest against your values?

If you don't want to invest in tobacco or alcohol or gambling, or you don't want to own any shares in fossil fuels, that's going to significantly limit your opportunities in superannuation or other forms of investment.

My spicy opinion on this is: I think it's actually okay to hold things in your super fund that aren't in line with your values, if you know that there's a long-term strategy at play. I also think we need to recognise that there's a lot of privilege that comes with having the ability to invest ethically.

For instance, I have a client who inherited a significant parcel of shares from his grandfather. They happen to be BHP shares and they were bought so long ago, they were purchased with British pound sterling. They've compounded in value over time and they pay strong dividends, so from an investment perspective, they deliver. However, from an ethical perspective, my client was interested in selling the shares.

The problem: the capital gains on those shares over such a long period of time means that if he sells them, he's up for a very significant amount of money in CGT. So much money that it's genuinely not worth it.

It made no sense to sell down the asset when he didn't need the cash, paying a shitload of CGT along the way, to invest in another asset that would be worth less – all because of a values misalignment.

Now, knowing his values, I'm not going to help him buy *new* BHP shares. But I'm also not going to recommend that he sell his existing BHP shares, because the money he's making from them can be put to good use, by investing the dividends from the BHP fund into a new, ethical fund. What we've done is counterbalanced his portfolio by paying into a fund that *is* in alignment with his values, and he now feels like he's putting BHP's money towards saving the Great Barrier Reef.

I believe wholeheartedly that ethical investing is the way of the future, and I'm really excited about that. But this story is a reminder: it's often much more complicated than a straight-up, binary choice.

ACTIVIST INVESTING

An activist investor is a shareholder who has an equity stake in a company that they use to put pressure on its management. For example, an investor (who usually has a whole heap of cash behind them!) might purchase a really large number of shares in a company with the precise intention of influencing the board and leadership team to make changes to their operations.

While this might be the first time you're encountering the term, activist investing isn't a new concept – it actually had a peak in 2014. An example you might have heard of was when Yahoo changed its bylaws to allow certain investors to nominate up to 20 per cent of its board, following the actions of a group of activist investors.

How to actually ethically invest

'But Victoria, how do I literally DO ethical investing?'

When it comes to finding the right investment for you, what's great is it's much easier than it was ten years ago, because all of the big investment houses now have ESG options.

Each investor has their own way of approaching the process but, broadly, once you've decided what's important to you, you apply 'screens' to individual businesses.

- **Negative screens** are for certain types of companies you plan to exclude in your portfolio.
- **Positive screens** are for those companies you're aiming to include in your portfolio.

For instance, if you decide that tobacco or dairy farms or fossil fuels are not in alignment with your values, then you can deliberately avoid putting them in your portfolio. It's as simple as setting a criteria, like my nuclear weapons client.

Once the screen has been established, it helps you find a fund that identifies companies that do not meet this ESG criteria. They can then be excluded from your list.

Traditionally, ESG-managed funds and ETFs only use negative screening, so they rely on filtering out the businesses that *don't* align with their values. Meanwhile, positive screening is generally focused on including companies with strong ESG characteristics.

When you're positive screening, you're looking for companies that are actively making the world a better place. You might choose to support businesses in the education sector, those who are delivering necessities like clean water or housing, or perhaps companies investing in environmental technology. The choice is ultimately yours.

YOUR SCREENING CRITERIA

Note down a few of the things you think you'd like to rule out or rule in to your portfolio. What's a 'hell yes' to you – and what's a 'hell no'?

Negative screens	Positive screens

If you're a micro investor, platforms like Raiz and Spaceship have socially responsible portfolios as well. For example, both of those platforms have ESG options that seek to match investments with personal values and provide exposure to large ESG Australian and global companies.

You can also buy ESG ETFs very easily, and most share platforms are becoming very responsive to consumers' growing preference to weed out options based on ethical considerations.

There's a lot of self-regulation or self-reflection involved, but to be honest it doesn't really add that much extra time or effort to the research process. And I believe it's important to take this step, to ensure your investments line up with your values.

And remember, friends: just as there are countless green-washed brands in supermarkets, with products that look eco-friendly but are actually toxic and unfriendly to the earth, there are portfolios and investment opportunities that use greenwashing, too. They use the right words and celebrate the right 'days' and they seem to be committed to ethical practices and outcomes, but with very little regulation in this space, it's hard to prove they're actually walking the walk. You need to use your own nous to understand whether it's a ruse, or something that is genuinely going to make a positive impact. But you've got this!

RESPONSIBLE RETURNS

An initiative of the RIAA, Responsible Returns is a tool you can use for free to assist you in finding out about financial products that apply a responsible or ethical investment strategy.[20]

RIAA champions responsible investing and a sustainable financial system, and is dedicated to ensuring capital is aligned with achieving a healthy society, environment and economy.

With over 350 members managing more than AU$9 trillion in assets globally, RIAA represents the largest and most active network of people and organisations engaged in responsible, ethical and impact investing in Australia and New Zealand.

● ● ● ● ● ●

ZOE, 20 – VIC

I would like to be invested in an ethical (sustainable) portfolio, but the only sustainable one my super offers is not high growth, which I want my super to be as I am young. Right now, I invest about 50–50 Australian shares and international shares. My shares outside super are also in an ethical fund that doesn't invest in fossil fuels and tobacco.

JOCELYN, 22 – ACT

I have invested in ETFs, but I did it too soon, before I knew about things like dollar cost averaging or ethical investing. I am glad that I have done it, but I wish I could go back and start again. I went off the principle that time in the market is better than timing the market, and I put a lump sum in at once. I also invested in a few ETFs that aren't necessarily aligned with my values, as they include companies I don't necessarily want to support. I just did not know what to look for and how to make those decisions! Instead, I looked for reliable, popular performers that were spread across a few different markets. Because I invested at the peak of the market, I didn't want to withdraw. I would rather gradually increase my investment in ETFs that do align with my values.

KAY, 34 – NSW

I have my super with Hesta on the ethical package. I see money as a vote, and it's important for me to vote for the best outcomes for the environment, so I want to be sure I am not contributing to coal, logging and mining.

● ● ● ● ● ●

TAKE NOTE

Ethical investing is not heavily regulated.

....

It means different things to different people and when thinking about it you can consider your own personal beliefs and values.

....

Ethical investments can out-perform traditional investments, so it can be a good move for the planet *and* your finances.

....

You can use both positive and negative screens to set the guidelines for how you choose to 'ethically invest'.

....

Chapter 9

Get savvy about super

Super can be a bit of a secret weapon in your investment portfolio, and I want to show you how!

What super is and how to choose the right fund were covered in my first book, *She's on the Money*, so we're not going to go over too many basics here. Instead, in this chapter, I'll be focusing on how super exists as an investment for your future wealth, and how we can ensure we're utilising this investment tool in the best way possible.

Now, I'm going to be straight up: if you're relying on your superannuation and government pension to look after you in retirement . . . you're screwed. It's simply not enough.

As mentioned in Chapter 1, the Association of Superannuation Funds of Australia (ASFA) calculates that a single person will need $46,494 a year to live comfortably throughout their retirement, with couples calculated to need $65,445 a year.

Alternatively, they recommend you have a pot of around $545,000 for a single or $640,000 for a couple at retirement which, when you do the math, will only be sufficient for nine to 12 years. Hmmmm! So they're basically encouraging you to retire at 65 or 67 with enough income to last you around a decade, a little more if you're investing that capital and getting a small return . . . and then what? Then, if you have very little wealth or assets behind you, you might qualify for the pension, which is currently around $25,000 a year for a single person, and a little over $19,000 each for a couple.

This recommendation is also built on the assumption that the retirees own their own home (with no mortgage) which, as we discussed in Chapter 7, isn't a priority or even a possibility for some people.

Then there's the fact that we're also living for longer. The average life expectancy is up, now around 82 years.[21] We have an ageing population that is increasingly likely to live even beyond that, thanks to medical and wellness innovations. In fact, I saw a statistic recently that confirmed we currently live in a world where a person might live up to 150 years![22]

Let that sink in for a moment. The average retirement age is between 65 and 70, but future generations could live to be *twice* that age. How on earth will they support themselves for all those decades after they finish working?

Let's get one thing straight: superannuation exists to support the government by relieving financial pressure on the public purse. Obviously, it's there to support you, too, but it's really important for you to understand that the government cannot afford to look after all of us in our twilight years. So, super was created to encourage us to pay for our retirement ourselves.

A lot of other countries don't have the same level of social support as Australia does when it comes to universal health care, paid parental leave, study payments and general support payments for those who are unemployed.

So I think that people can fall into the trap of expecting the best from our government. They take the attitude of, 'They're going to look after us in retirement, don't worry!' As a result, these people don't make the concept of saving for retirement into any kind of priority. And that opens up a HUGE risk for later in life.

The super guarantee is increasing over the next few years to put us in a better position. It was at 9 per cent for a very long time, it then increased to 9.5 per cent, then again to 10.5 per cent in July 2022. It's due to keep increasing by 0.5 per cent each year until it reaches 12 per cent from 1 July 2025. But in my view, as an adviser, I believe even those amounts aren't going to keep up with inflation, and they're certainly not going to pay for a financially comfortable retirement.

Super is the government's way of saying it's up to *you* to create your own secure financial future.

Guess what? You're an investor

Many people think they can't afford to invest, but guess what? Since you started working, you've already been investing 9–10 per cent of your income.

If you're 35, you've already been investing for potentially 20 years if, like me, you got your first part-time job when you were a teenager. (Ah, the memories.) I can pinpoint the day that I was handed my first superannuation form. I had been employed at a very popular ice cream shop on the Mornington Peninsula. I walked in for my very first shift and was handed an employment pack, which included forms for my emergency contacts and bank details, and a super form.

At that point in time, I don't think I'd ever even talked about super before, let alone knew what it was or why it mattered. I had to go home and ask my parents what it meant. I was a bit confused: why did they want to take 9.5 per cent of my income and lock it away in an account I couldn't touch for another 50 years?

As I've mentioned, my dad's an accountant. I remember the conversation, because he told me how important it was and how impactful compounding is. Basically, the money invested in my super at the tender age of 15 could be worth hundreds of thousands of dollars by the time I retired, he explained.

It all sounded great, but I remember going through the form and having absolutely no clue when it came to which fund to choose or how they were different. The way it was explained to me was, I would only get paid super if I worked over a certain amount of hours per month. And none of the nuts and bolts of what super actually was, was ever made clear.

I really wish someone had sat me down and explained the concept of investing. I also wish they'd explained that super itself isn't an investment: it's a tax vehicle. When you have a super fund, that allows you to invest inside that tax vehicle. You don't actually ever invest in 'superannuation'; you invest in a super fund, which then invests in shares, companies and funds on your behalf. Some of the things they put your money in could be investments you make as a personal investor – it's just much more tax effective to do it through your super fund.

As I touched on way back in Chapter 3, super is the closest thing we have to a tax haven in Australia. It gives you real sexy tax rates, especially if you're in a higher marginal tax bracket, as it is a structure that's enabled us to have a tax rate of just 15 per cent.

So how does it all work?

Superannuation in a nutshell

Say you started investing at the age of 21, and you invested $500 each and every month into a share portfolio that had an average rate of return of 7.5 per cent. By the age of 60, that share portfolio might be worth $1.25 million.

Of that $1.25 million, just $234,000 was your regular contributions. The other $1 million was all investment returns. You've made a million dollars just by being in the market for that period.

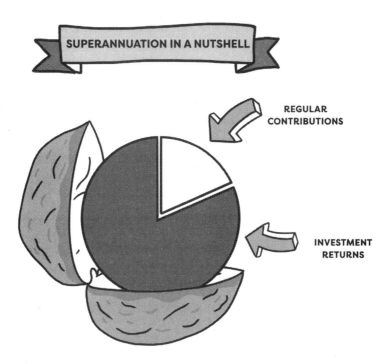

SUPERANNUATION IN A NUTSHELL

REGULAR
CONTRIBUTIONS

INVESTMENT
RETURNS

Superannuation was introduced to give every Australian this type of opportunity to set themselves up for a financially secure future.

Now, as you know by now, investing isn't a straight line forward. Your money doesn't grow in value year after year after year; it zigzags. It goes up one year (or month, or week, or day, or hour!), down the next, flatlines for a bit, then grows again . . .

This is why time in the market is so valuable, as I keep saying. If you hold your money in an investment class for long enough, you're more likely to withstand all of the down periods and enjoy the profits of the growth periods, so you come out on top.

Superannuation is paid automatically by your employer. As of 1 July 2022, every single employee over the age of 18 is eligible to receive super, regardless of their age, how many hours they work, whether they're casual, part-time or full-time. Which I think is fantastic! This wasn't always the case, as there used to be all sorts of criteria and benchmarks you had to meet in order to get paid super.

As of 1 July 2022, the amount of super you're entitled to is 10.5 per cent of your income. So if your earnings before tax are $1000 a week, you're entitled to receive 10.5 per cent, or $105, deposited into your super fund at the same time.

That money is then invested according to the strategy you've chosen within your fund. This is your superannuation guarantee, but you can also choose to add your own voluntary contributions (more on that below).

Your super investment strategy

'But Victoria, hold up! I never chose a strategy. I have no idea what my fund invests in.'

If you're thinking this, it's likely you've chosen a default super fund, which usually invests in a balanced, low-risk fund.

There are generally four different kinds of investment 'risk profiles' you can nominate within your super fund: conservative funds, balanced, growth or high growth.

Conservative funds are relatively low risk, and also aim for low returns.

Balanced funds are the most common or popular, because they aim for slightly higher returns than conservative funds, but without too much greater risk.

Growth funds are going to see you take some risks with your money, but the returns could be much higher.

High growth funds are the riskiest of the bunch, but can achieve the highest returns and profits.

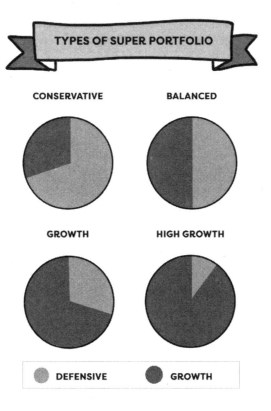

The right type of investment strategy in your super fund aligns with your investment strategy overall (if you need to, head back to Chapter 3 on risk for a refresher). But when it comes to super, you also have to consider your age.

If you're 25 and you have 40 years left in the workforce, you may be able to afford to invest in a growth or high growth fund, because you have plenty of income-earning years ahead of you. Over the next 40 years, your fund can weather the ups and downs of a riskier strategy because you have plenty of time ahead of you for your returns to compound and grow. If you invest in a company that has a massive downturn, for instance, it's not the end of the world, because you still have decades to recoup that loss.

On the other hand, if you are in your fifties or sixties and knocking on retirement's door in the near-ish future, it might make more sense to adopt a lower-risk strategy. A balanced fund could offer you the chance to enjoy some solid profits, without the risk of a big downturn chipping away at your retirement wealth.

A COUPLE OF THOUGHTS ON CHOOSING A SUPER FUND

- If you pay peanuts, you might get monkeys. You want a good super fund that supports your goals and has really good returns. Don't just go with the cheapest fund without considering performance, and always remember that past performance isn't an indicator of how the fund will perform in the future.
- Compare apples with apples when looking at fees. It's incredibly important to understand that all of the companies charge fees differently. Some might have a management fee, some have a funds management fee, some charge an administration fee, others charge a percentage of what you contribute each year. Make sure you look for the total sum of all the fees when comparing funds.

Fund types

As well as the type of investment strategy, the other decision you should make is the type of fund you want. There are literally dozens of super funds to choose from, and they all charge different fees and achieve different investment returns on your money.

The main types of super funds to choose from are:

Industry funds: These funds usually focus on a particular industry, like retail or hospitality, but they're open to all Australians. If you've ever worked for a restaurant or cafe, there's a good chance you have (or had) a HostPlus Super policy. Another big one is Australian Super. All profits they make go back into the fund to benefit new and existing members.

Retail funds: These are funds that are owned by a bank, insurance provider or another large financial institution. They are for-profit funds, so any profits they make are split between members and shareholders. Examples include BT Super (owned by Westpac) and Colonial First State (owned by CommBank).

Member-owned funds: These are similar to industry funds, however, they're not part of the official Industry Super Funds group. Plus, some of these funds might be reserved for people in a particular state or industry – like UniSuper, for example, which provides superannuation services to employees within the higher education and research sector in Australia. With over 450,000 members, it's got a cool $100 billion in assets.

Setting up a fund

Now, you might be reading along right now, thinking, 'This all seems difficult and boring, but the stakes seem too high for me to park it in the "too hard" basket any longer.'

If so, you're like a huge chunk of Australians who switch off when it comes to super. You're not alone, so don't beat yourself up about it. I'm proud of you for taking the proactive choice of reading this book – we can fix this!

This may sound complicated, but honestly, these are decisions you only have to make once. To set up your fund, you simply need to:

1. Find the fund that best suits your needs and goals. It's a bit of work and I'd recommend seeing an adviser BUT if you want to DIY, I suggest looking at the super comparison tool on the ATO website. *Make sure that the fund offers the risk profile that suits you!*
2. Apply for a new fund – this takes a couple of minutes and can be done online.
3. Roll all of your existing funds into it – you can do a rollover from your MyGov account: see box below for more on this!
4. Then simply revisit your fund every year or two, to make sure the choices you've made still align with your goals.

DON'T BE LIKE YOUNG VICTORIA

When I was first starting out in finance, I sat down with an adviser and had a chat about my super, and they recommended an organisation-specific super fund. Their parting words? 'Make sure you consolidate all your other super funds into this one.'

Do you think I did it? Of course I didn't. Despite the fact that I was working in finance? And even though I knew that all of those fees were eroding my eventual wealth? Crazy, isn't it?

The reason I didn't consolidate my funds was because I just didn't know how to do it. It turns out, I'm not alone – according to the ATO, around 12 million Australians have one super account, and around 4 million people hold two or more super accounts. That's millions upon millions of dollars in additional fees being spent every single month – money that's far better off in those individuals' pockets!

To be honest, I was confused and thought the process of consolidating my super would be tedious, time-consuming and complex. In reality, it's one of the easiest things to do. It takes about three minutes on the myGov website and the super fund will do most of the work for you, after submitting your forms.[23]

I had been paying double fees for a good ten years (a full decade!) before I finally consolidated my funds, and I shudder to think how many tens of thousands of dollars Future Victoria is going to miss out on, because Young Victoria didn't get her shit together.

Don't be like me.

If you have more than one super fund, work out which one aligns with your goals and is working hardest for you, and consolidate all of the other accounts into that fund. It's the most money you'll ever make in the space of a few minutes.

THE DIFFERENCE CONSOLIDATING YOUR SUPER ACCOUNTS CAN MAKE

According to the
ASIC Money Smart superannuation calculator

1 SUPER ACCOUNT

$100 annually in fees

$250 annually in insurance

$14,000 IN FEES*

AFTER 40 YEARS

5 SUPER ACCOUNTS

$100 annually in fees

$250 annually in insurance

$70,000 IN FEES*

AFTER 40 YEARS

* IN TODAY'S DOLLARS

Consolidating your super accounts

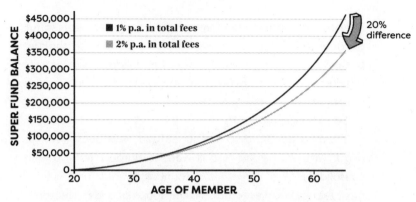

Impact of fees upon your end retirement benefit
(Source: Rainmaker Information)

Why would you add extra to your super?

Say you got an inheritance or a tax refund. Or you've been doing your budget and you want to invest and grow your wealth, and you reckon you have an extra $50–100 a week you could afford to put somewhere, but you're not quite sure what to do with it?

This is where you might want to consider adding extra to your super.

For example, I once had a client couple who received a decent inheritance from a family member overseas who passed away. The amount wasn't 'quit our jobs, we're going to live off our dividends on a yacht in Cannes' money, but it was enough that they wanted to think really long and hard about how they invested it.

In the end, we decided to establish a super fund. But here's the trick: we established the fund in the name of their brand-new baby, which you are legally allowed to do for a minor. This couple dumped the whole inheritance in that super fund and we projected that by the time their child turned 65, the fund could be worth around $4 million.

Can you imagine being able to set your child up for a successful future like this? Or perhaps even set yourself up?!

This is why it's so important that you know what opportunities you have with super and, just as crucially, you know what your rights are when it comes to what you can access and what you can't.

Take my client's example above. This is an incredible projected outcome, but we also have to take into account:

- The chance that the final profit might fall short of our projections.
- The risks associated with the specific investments in the fund.
- The fact that superannuation rules and policies could change over time.
- The biggest one: the fact that this money is locked away for decades, and my client can only access it under very specific conditions.

I highlight all of these aspects for you because I think it's really important to consider the good and the bad when investing extra money in your super.

Some people put pressure on themselves to add more to superannuation, but you need to look at the bigger picture of what your personal situation is. If you're saying to yourself, 'I really want to add more money to my super, but I also have this personal loan . . .', then putting extra money into super is probably not a good idea, because you're prioritising a long-term result over a short-term outcome.

Sometimes, our short-term goals really do need to take priority. As I've already mentioned, paying off debt is an investment in itself, and it's crucial to remember that building your financial future is something you should be working towards without sacrificing your current situation.

Keep in mind, too, that just because you might not be in a position to contribute extra to your superannuation today doesn't mean you won't *ever* contribute more to super. Who knows what the future holds!

Okay, so let's say you *do* want to add extra to your super – even if it's starting with just $20 a week. How does that work in practice?

In the simplest terms, when you make super contributions, they are either concessional or non-concessional.

Concessional contributions are contributions that you deposit into your super fund *before* you pay any tax. Ordinarily they are then taxed at a rate of just 15 per cent.

If you earn a salary and pay more than 15 per cent tax, which, right now, is anyone who earns more than $18,000, then this is a tax advantage. For example:

You earn $100,000 before tax. You make a concessional additional superannuation contribution of $10,000 per year. Instead of paying $3,250 income tax on that $10,000 income, you pay $1500 tax on your super contribution. You are $1750 better off immediately – and we haven't even factored in the growth of your investments over time!

There is a limit to how much you can contribute to your super fund in this way. From 1 July 2022, the concessional contributions cap is $27,500 a year.

The ATO confirms that your personal cap may be higher if you didn't use the full amount of your cap in earlier years. This is called the carry-forward of unused concessional contributions. Unused cap amounts are available to carry forward for five years, after which they expire.

Note: You can salary sacrifice into your superannuation, which means you take money you've earned and before you pay any tax on it, you deposit it into your super fund. The big benefit is that in most cases you'll only pay 15 per cent tax on that money when you deposit it, which is likely to be far less than the tax you pay on your regular income. The downside is that the money is now locked away in your super fund until retirement, so it's not liquid or accessible cash.

Warning: If you do salary sacrifice into your super, it doesn't actually impact your HECS repayments. Your HECS is calculated on how much you're meant to get, including superannuation, not how much you *actually* get.

The last thing I want is for you to get bill shock when a big HECS invoice lands in your mailbox! So keep this in mind.

Non-concessional contributions are contributions that you deposit into your super fund *after* paying tax – for example, they're paid from after-tax pay or from savings. They therefore include any personal contributions you make into your super account that aren't claimed as tax deductions. If you've made a contribution to your superannuation fund from your take-home pay, you might be able to claim it at tax time so it becomes a non-concessional contribution.

A word on the super gap

Two months. Sixty-one days. Nearly nine weeks.

No matter how you put it, the fact is that the average Australian woman has to work 61 days more than a man per year in order to take home the same pay packet.

There's even a day each year to mark the occasion – 31 August is Equal Pay Day in Australia, to denote the 61 additional days women have to work (from the start of the financial year) to earn the same amount as their male counterparts.

These figures are averages, of course, but they speak to a wider problem. In general, women earn less than men. Which means they're going to retire with less super than a guy *who is doing the exact same job.*

Before I dig into this (and believe me, we *are* digging in), I'm keen to define straight up what this means. I've seen a bit of confusion around what the difference is between the super gap, the pay gap and the gender pay gap – understandably, I think! – so let's clear it up.

The **super gap** is the difference between what the average Australian retires with in their super account, based on their gender. There are various figures out there in different reports and for different age brackets, but according to KPMG, the median superannuation balance for men aged 60–64 years is $204,107, whereas for women in the same age group, it is $146,900 – a difference of over $67,000.[24]

The **gender pay gap** is the difference between the average pay that different genders earn. This is a general trend or set of statistics, and relates to the community as a whole.

A **pay gap** is literally the gap that exists between two individuals doing the exact same role. It has nothing to do with gender.

They're separate but intrinsically linked issues, because when we're looking at a pay gap, and especially a gender pay gap, it's clear that women, on average, contribute less to super over their working lives than men, simply because they're paid less.

There are loads of different movements, initiatives and campaigns designed to try and rectify this, which is really good. Some of them are helping to move the needle towards a time where men and women performing the same job will be paid equally. But we still have a really long way to go . . .

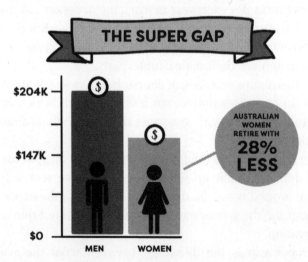

One area I think we need to make huge progress on is around pay secrecy. I believe people are smart enough to understand that different roles require different skill sets, and different rates of pay are fairly allocated (at least in theory) as a result. It's also the case that the individual experience and expertise you have can influence how much you're paid.

I cannot wrap my head around pay secrecy policies, where businesses go out of their way to add clauses to employment contracts to prevent staff from talking about how much money they earn. Why would any company who is doing the right thing by their employees prevent their employees from having the freedom to have that comparison?

I think I just answered my own question there!

This is a bit of a spicy topic, and whenever I talk about it on my social media or when I'm interviewed for a story, it stirs up a *lot* of feedback.

'I don't have to tell anyone what I'm getting paid!'

'I shouldn't have to share my salary details with anyone!'

'Why should I tell you how much I earn?'

To be super clear, I'm not suggesting companies should publish individual names and salaries, so everyone knows what Jinnie in marketing and Ralph in accounts are earning down to the dollar.

But I *am* a big fan of a more general style of sharing employment buckets and salary bands. It could simply be a document that indicates that this role typically sits between $X and $Y remuneration. A starting point like this could make a massive impact for people as they get comfortable asking for more money, as they grow in their careers. Right now, these are conversations we should be having: how much is this role worth? How much more does that promotion pay? The fundamental lack of transparency around income is contributing to the whole issue of gender pay gaps.

A really big piece of the puzzle is people knowing their worth, which is something I'm super passionate about. But how do you know your worth if no one's allowed to tell you? It shouldn't be a conversation that is thwarted by your employer – it should be encouraged.

Let me tell you about a friend of mine who works in the media. She's part of the executive team and had been sitting on an internal committee for two years when there was an internal restructure and some roles shifted around.

She was juggling too many balls, so she asked a colleague if he wanted to step in and take over her role on the committee.

'Are you sure?' he said. 'Won't you miss the ten grand?'

What ten grand?

It turned out that executives who sat on the committee at this particular organisation were usually paid $10,000 per year for doing so.

No one had ever told her about it and she'd never received it. But you can bet your last dollar that the seven men on the committee were banking their bonuses!

This is what happens when we don't encourage these open conversations: we don't know what to ask for. We don't know what we're worth.

The end result for businesses is that we become disheartened, overwhelmed and exhausted, and we don't give them the productivity and output they could get if they just paid us the same rate they do men.

The end result for women is that we retire with significantly less money in our super accounts than our male counterparts.

What can you do about the super pay gap in terms of your own financial picture? Here are my hot tips:

- Make a plan to contribute a few per cent more to super on a regular basis, if you can.
- Negotiate your salary with your employer.
- Be active in picking the right fund for you, because while we don't chase performance, performance really matters over the long term.
- Ensure you're invested in line with the right risk profile for you and that you're happy with it.

- Ensure you understand the fees on your fund.
- Talk to your employer about your maternity leave and whether they will still pay super during this time.
- Before going on parental leave, contact your super fund to see if they can waive the fees while you're not working.
- If you're on extended parental leave, have a conversation with your partner about them potentially contributing to your super fund while you're not earning an income.
- If you're planning to work overseas for any period of time, consider still contributing to super while you're away.
- Know your worth!

Is it ever too late to get started?

Some of the most heartbreaking stories I hear from our community are when someone reaches out and says, 'I think it's too late for me.' They might be in their fifties, starting again after divorce; or in their forties, realising that they haven't paid any attention to their super fund or retirement plans or building for their financial future in any way, shape or form. And now, they're worried they've missed the boat.

If this resonates with you, I want you to know: it's *never* too late.

If you're a late bloomer when it comes to getting your financial ducks in a row, don't despair – it doesn't mean it's not possible. It's *always* possible to put yourself in a better financial position than you were.

If you're in your fifties and you're able to really create a strategy and prioritise super a little bit more, that could mean an extra $100 a week or $5,000 a year that goes into your fund over the next decade. That's another $50,000 in capital you're adding to your retirement fund. This could put you in a position where you potentially have $100,000 more in your retirement bucket.

The smallest changes can have an impact. Even an extra $200 a month in retirement income can mean a better standard of living, and you can create that outcome by making some small shifts and adjustments to your budget and lifestyle now. You're probably not going to be a millionaire, and this isn't a get-rich-quick book (and I never ever set out for it to be that!). I believe in get rich *slow*.

But if you haven't been afforded the opportunity of financial literacy earlier on in your life, or you haven't really understood or connected with investing, that's okay. That's your journey. But it's never too late to make a positive change.

It's never too late to know what good budgeting and cash flow is, and to get your super sorted. The worst thing you could do is to keep your head in the sand and hope things improve, without actually having a plan to get there.

The bottom line? You can't rely on anybody else for this, so take this as your call to arms to get in the driver's seat and work out exactly what's possible.

SUPER CHECK-IN

To get your super in tip-top shape, check out these free tools online that allow you to calculate and project your super into the future, comparing the impact of different contributions and investments.

Search for any lost super here: superfundlookup.gov.au

Compare super options here: ato.gov.au/Calculators-and-tools/YourSuper-comparison-tool

Get help choosing the right super fund here: moneysmart.gov.au/how-super-works/choosing-a-super-fund

Project your super balance for the future here: moneysmart.gov.au/how-super-works/superannuation-calculator

● ● ● ● ● ●

STEPHANIE, 31 – VIC

Honestly, I wasn't taught finance in schooling or home. So credit cards were fun. They gave me holidays and I lived out of my means. That's something that took a bit of adjusting to and took years to pay off. So I have taught myself everything. Started with shame to give me a kick in the butt, as I was in debt, playing the comparison game. But I knuckled down and I'm now out of debt with $35,000 savings, $100,000 super and $4,000 in shares!

TARA, 37 – WA

My main value in terms of super is to make bulk money and it's performed well for me. But I disassociate a bit with it, because I don't see it as my money, even though it is. I don't actually care about what it is invested in as long as the bottom line is good. Probably a little irresponsible to the world, though, as it holds the bulk of my wealth and could make more of a difference . . .

STEPH, 24 – NSW

I need to look into my super more. I only consolidated it into one account earlier this year, but that's all I really know about it at the moment! My investment strategy right now is to invest $150 per week into one platform, then $1,000–2,000 every few months into a second one, but I don't have a very strict strategy yet.

● ● ● ● ● ●

TAKE NOTE

You are responsible for funding your
retirement. So get savvy about it!

....

Super itself isn't an investment but rather a tax vehicle. When you
have a super fund, it allows you to invest inside that tax vehicle.

....

Make sure you're comparing apples with apples
when you compare super funds, and don't necessarily
base your choice on the lowest fees.

....

Chapter 10

Empowered direct investing

So far we've looked at the fundamentals of the investing journey. But, knowing the She's on the Money community and how keen you are, how quick to learn, I think it's quite possible that you may want to try more direct investing by yourself; let's say if you want to become an informed investor who makes individual, personalised decisions about how to build your wealth in the share market. This chapter is going to cover more of what will be helpful to understand *before* taking that step.

That said, if you want to invest in an ETF or you have an adviser who can guide you, you might not need to get too deeply involved in the numbers and the details. And that's totally fine – you can continue on your investment journey as you are.

Yep, this is my way of saying, if you're not yet ready for direct investing and you don't want to go into all the detail that I've laid out in this chapter, then you can flick through it. Give yourself a free pass! You can always come back to it in the future.

However, if you're feeling curious, and are up for some deeper-diving into the workings and output of the businesses you're considering investing in, before you get involved in building a portfolio of shares there are other steps you can take. It's not just a case of 'Afterpay seems to be doing well! I should buy some shares!' It's about digging into the details to find out how a company is performing, and how it's expecting to perform in the future.

I interviewed a 22-year-old recently. And when I asked her, 'What do you invest in?' she replied that she'd invested in three companies directly and in some ETFs.

'How did you know how to pick those specific companies?' I enquired.

Her reply was surprising, but not uncommon: via a recommendation from a colleague. 'I work in mining. The boys on-site said that that's what they would buy, so I followed their lead.'

To be clear: that wasn't genuine financial advice! But because it seemed like a good idea, she went out and bought shares and invested her hard-won money into those specific shares, based on the recommendation of someone who may or may not know what they're talking about.

This is not the ideal way to build your wealth!

We have to be so careful. My interviewee's workmates didn't have any professional experience in the financial advice space – *professional* being the key here. They might have been investors for years, but that doesn't mean her colleagues know how to take into consideration the important things we've discussed in this book such as values, goals, needs, risk profiles and diversification. Thankfully, the person I interviewed didn't make a bad decision; it was a relatively safe choice, and she did well out of those investments. But ideally you want to make these decisions from your own informed, unbiased place, not because someone random in your life recommended it.

COGNITIVE BIASES

A cognitive bias is a faulty or skewed way of thinking that occurs when we're trying to process information from the world around us and make misinterpretations based on the information we have, think we have, or actually don't have at all!

Cognitive biases occur all the time and can crop up in all areas of life, but some can particularly come into play in the world of finance and investing. Here are a few to look out for:

- **Narrative fallacy:** choosing less favourable outcomes due to the fact that they have a good story behind them. As humans, we're hooked in by strong narratives that make sense to us.
- **Framing cognitive bias:** basing an investment decision on how the information is framed or presented to us.
- **Herd mentality:** blindly copying what other investors are doing, particularly famous investors. Emotion overcomes independent analysis.
- **Overconfidence bias:** overestimation of our talent, skill or self-belief, which means we make decisions based on an inflated sense of confidence in our abilities.
- **Self-serving bias:** when we think that a positive outcome is down to our own skill or ability but a negative outcome is just down to bad luck.
- **Confirmation bias:** seeking out information and advice that affirms and reinforces views and ideas we already hold, and avoiding anything that contradicts them.

Can you think of a time when you've been subject to one of these biases with your personal finances?

So, what kind of information can you uncover to help you decide which companies you might be best investing in? Let's look at what I would say are the most important things to take a squiz at before you part with any of your cash in this way. With everything that follows, it's about looking for signs that a company is in good health, being well managed and is likely to perform well financially to return strong growth and/or dividends to its shareholders. Basically, a better chance of making bank!

How to read an annual report

If you're anything like me, you'll love nothing more than the opportunity to get stuck into a company's annual report, spending hours up to your eyeballs in the details of what said company does, why it does it and how it makes its money. But you're probably nothing like me! So this prospect may well seem tedious and intimidating and time-consuming.

I'm not going to sugar-coat it: reading a company's annual report means digging into quite detailed documents. I wouldn't describe it as beach reading! But it's research that really pays off. An annual report is the main big document that a company uses to communicate details of its activities, financial results and strategies to shareholders and other stakeholders. Companies will release one every year (as you've probably guessed from the name). The annual report of ASX-listed companies includes some material that is legally required, such as:

● A director's report: with information that company shareholders would reasonably require to make an informed assessment of the company, its strategies and financial position.

● A corporate governance statement: which discloses the extent to which a company has followed non-mandatory guidelines of the ASX, or explains why it has not done so.

- A financial statement: which provides people who are interested in the company with information about its financial performance and financial position.
- A remuneration report: outlining and explaining the pay of the company executives, including bonuses and commission, and how this relates to the business's performance.
- An auditor's report: an independent accounting practitioner's assessment and opinion of both the financial report and the remuneration report.

As I said: we're talking lengthy documents . . . like, 180 pages or so!

So, what's the purpose of these big reports and why do you need to review them? In a nutshell, they help you as an investor understand a company's overall health and its profit prospects for the future. And they help you answer important questions such as: is the company in debt? How much debt? What is its income like – has it been growing? What have the risks to revenue been?

Basically, these reports are an indication of a company's overall strength as a business. If you plan to invest in a particular company, it's essential to review its latest annual report as a starting point to understand where the company stands now, and where it's going in the future.

Hot tip: Keep in mind that the annual report will be written by members of that company, and that it also functions as a marketing tool for attracting potential investors, so we need to consume it with a grain of salt. It's a really useful jumping-off point, though.

What is a financial statement?

A financial statement is a report that shows the business activities and financial performance of a business. It includes things like:

- a balance sheet;
- an income statement;
- a cash flow statement;
- a statement of changes in equity (retained earnings).

When reviewing a financial statement, you want to look out for things like:

- Debt load: debt isn't necessarily a bad thing, depending on how a company uses it. But if a business is borrowing too much, debt load could be worth considering.
- Cash flow trends: is the company's net income much higher than its cash flow? Try to find out why. If a company has low cash flow for 11 months of the year, and then one massively successful month, what's behind that? Is it a seasonal business (like a Christmas tree farm!) or is it just not performing for 11 months of the year?
- Earnings and revenue growth: this will tell you whether a company is on a growth trajectory or in decline. This data is usually easiest to find in the reports or simply from the company's press releases announcing the results.

What is a balance sheet?

A balance sheet is basically a snapshot of a business's financial condition at a single point in time. It contains the business's assets, liabilities and owner's (shareholders') equity at that time.[25] You might also hear it referred to as the 'statement of financial position' – same thing.

Here's what a balance sheet might look like – this is a real-world example from Apple in the US:

Assets	2018
Current Assets US$ millions	
Cash	45,059
Accounts receivable	14,324
Inventory	7,662
Prepaid expenses	20,127
Short-term investments	42,881
Total current assets	130,053
Non Current Assets ($)	
Lease receivables	
Property, plant, and equipment	35,077
(Less accumulated depreciation	
Long term marketable securities	179,286
Total fixed assets	214,363
Other Assets ($)	
Deferred income tax	
Other	23,086
Total other assets	23,086
Total Assets ($)	**367,502**

Liabilities and Owner's Equity	
Current Liabilities ($)	
Accounts payable	34,311
Short-term loans	
Deferred income tax	7,775
Accrued salaries and wages	26,756
Commercial paper	11,980
Current portion of long-term debt	8,498
Total current liabilities	89,320
Long-term Liabilities ($)	
Long-term debt	101,362
Deferred income tax	3,087
Other non current liabilities	46,855
Total long-term liabilities	151,304

Equity Capital ($)	
Common stock	38,044
Retained earnings	91,898
Other comprehensive income loss	(3,064)
Total owner's equity	126,878
Non controlling interest	
Total Liabilities and Owner's Equity ($)	**367,502**

(Source: Apple SEC filings)

As you can see, the information is pretty top-line. Think of it this way: a restaurant's takeaway menu is a good representation of the ingredients in the kitchen, but it's not the full menu. For a more detailed picture, you turn to the annual report. But taking a look at the balance sheet is a great way to get a simple pulse check.

The assets side of the equation includes both cash and cash equivalents the business has, such as funds invested in a term deposit, along with the amount of money owed to the company by its customers. In short, it's what the company owns.

The liabilities side of the equation includes things like loans, bank account overdrafts, money owed to suppliers and payable tax. In short, it's what the company owes.

The most common formula for a balance sheet is A − L = E

Assets (owned) − Liabilities (owed) = Equity (worth)

Put simply, a balance sheet can show you how much a company is worth at the moment the snapshot is taken. Listed companies usually publish half-year and full-year financial reports.

What is an income statement?

So, we've established that a balance sheet reveals the position a company is in at a specific moment in time. By contrast, an income statement shows the company's revenues, costs and expenses over a period, and its resulting profit or loss (which is why it's sometimes referred to as a profit and loss statement).[26] This range of time is usually a year or a quarter (three months).

An income statement contains an overview of revenue, expenses, net income and earnings per share. Revenue is the money a company earns from the sale of its products and services. Some income statements may also include lines such as cost of goods sold (the costs directly tied to the product), and the gross profit (the amount of revenue available to pay for operational expenses and compensate ownership).

The main things to check for on an income statement are the total revenue amounts, total expenses and net income. Ideally, income should always exceed expenses to put the company in a profitable position. If it doesn't, we need to know why – because this could mean the company is going into debt.

What is a cash flow statement?

A business's cash flow relates to the net amount of cash, and cash equivalents, coming in and out over a period of time, usually 12 months. The cash-flow statement shows from where money is flowing in and to where it's going out.

Cash flow is different to profit. There could be cash flow of $20,000 coming in every week, but that doesn't equate to a profit of $20,000 per week. If the company's expenses are $18,000 a week, then the profit is only $2,000. In this case, a business could say they're making $1 million a year, which is technically accurate in terms of money coming in – but the real truth of the matter is that their profit is around $100,000 a year.

Cash flow is also distinct from revenue, which provides a measure of the effectiveness of a company's sales and marketing. Cash flow is more of a liquidity indicator.

Why is understanding cash flow important? Because it's about how the business manages its resources to function and to generate profits. The efficacy of a company's cash flow shows whether it can cover short-term expenses like bills and payroll. A company without a steady cash flow is likely to be heading into trouble, and even profitable companies can fail to manage their cash flow well.

When reviewing a business's cash flow, look out for the three major types of activity:

- Operating activities: cash flow that's generated once the company delivers its regular goods or services; this includes both revenue and expenses.
- Investing activities: cash flow from purchasing or selling assets; e.g. real estate, vehicles.
- Financing activities: cash flow from debt and equity financing.

As a potential investor, you want to see whether or not a company's cash from operating income exceeds its net income. This would indicate a positive cash flow and speaks to the company's ability to have greater assets than liabilities (meaning it is solvent), which suggests that it's in a position to continue to grow its operations and pay dividends.

Hot tip: A company's balance sheet, income statement and cash flow statement are often analysed and interpreted together because they show different things and each helps form a relatively complete picture of the health of the company.

Common terms of the trade

Are you still with me? I know it's quite a lot to absorb, so don't feel pressured to take on all this information immediately if it's new to you. It's an incremental process, and you'll get there! I used to read through this kind of stuff multiple times before I could get a good handle on it, so don't worry if it's the same for you – that's totally normal.

When you're ready, let's turn to some of what are called 'ratios', and other ways you would typically begin to understand, assess and compare a company's performance with a view to making an investment.

Ratios are basically one variable divided by another. You can use them to compare the same performance factor for a few different companies, or the same performance factor for one company at different points in time, to track how that company's been doing. It's always a good idea to consider multiple ratios together as that gives a fuller view of a business from a few angles.

There are numerous ratios, all with their uses, and I'm not going to throw them all at you now as I don't want to overwhelm you! Instead, we'll cover a few what are called 'profitability ratios' (net profit and return on assets, equity and investment) plus two 'solvency ratios' (debt-to-equity and interest coverage). As an investor, you want to get a fairly quick gauge on whether the company you're considering is making a profit and likely to continue doing so; and whether it can handle its long-term financial obligations such as debts.

The information you'll need to calculate these ratios can be found in the company's financial statements.

Net profit

The net profit margin is the relationship between a company's net income and its revenue, and tells you how much profit is generated from every $1 in sales. It's calculated by dividing the net income figure by the revenue figure, and then multiplying it by 100 to create a percentage. As you'd expect, ideally this percentage is high as that indicates a good profitability level.

For example, let's say a company's net income is $120,000 and its revenue is $400,000. If you divide $120,000 by $400,000 and multiply the result by 100, the result is a net profit margin of 30 per cent. This company is making 30 cents profit on every $1 in sales.

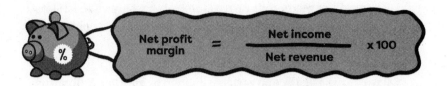

Net profit margin $=$ $\dfrac{\text{Net income}}{\text{Net revenue}}$ x 100

Once calculated, the net profit margin should be put into context. How does it compare to other companies within the same industry, and to those in other industries? And has it been decreasing or increasing for that company over time? Things like rising costs and changing market conditions can all have an impact on this ratio.

Return on assets (ROA)

The return on assets ratio is also a profitability ratio. It measures the net income produced by total assets during a period. Often called the 'return on total assets', it's essentially a measure of how much income was brought in by the company's assets.

It is calculated by dividing the company's net income by its total assets, expressed as a percentage. (Net profit can be found at the bottom of a company's income statement, and assets are found on its balance sheet.) For instance, if a company owns $10 million in assets and it brought in $1.5 million in income, the ROA would be 15 per cent.

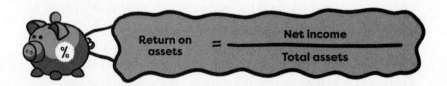

Return on assets $=$ $\dfrac{\text{Net income}}{\text{Total assets}}$

The point of an ROA is to measure how efficiently a company can manage its assets to produce profits. The higher the number, the better – this means the company is able to earn more money with a smaller investment. If an ROA reaches several dozen per cent, that's a great sign, but it is hard to, first, reach this level, and then to stay there. A good return on assets is considered about 10 to 15 per cent.[27]

Return on equity (ROE)

Some people think equity and assets are the same, but they're actually quite different. The ROE is another measure of how a company is doing financially; it is a profitability ratio that measures how effectively a company is making profits from its shareholders' investments.

To calculate ROE, analysts divide the company's net income by its average shareholders' equity. Because shareholders' equity equals assets minus liabilities, ROE is a measure of the return generated from the net assets of the company.

For example, a return of one means that every dollar of shareholders' equity makes $1 of net income. Potential investors want to see how efficiently a company uses its money to generate net income so this is an important metric for them.

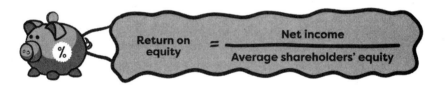

$$\text{Return on equity} = \frac{\text{Net income}}{\text{Average shareholders' equity}}$$

ROE also shows how well a company's management team is using equity financing to grow the company.

It's worth noting that ROE is a profitability ratio from the investor's point of view, not that of the company. So this ratio calculates how much money is being made based on the investment in the company, not via the company's investment in assets or whatever else.[28]

Return on investment (ROI)

ROI is another popular metric used for looking at a company's profitability; a ratio for figuring out how well an investment has performed – i.e. what gain or loss was made on a particular investment relative to its cost.

ROI is calculated by dividing the net income by the total cost of the investment, then multiplying by 100 to get a percentage.

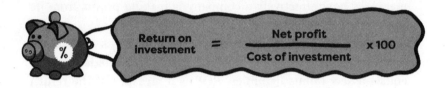

$$\text{Return on investment} = \frac{\text{Net profit}}{\text{Cost of investment}} \times 100$$

You're looking for a positive ROI as a starting point – that indicates a potential gain rather than loss. Its value as a measure comes when it's compared to the ROIs of other potential investments.

Debt to equity ratio

Now let's move on to our two debt ratios. This first one is a measure of how much debt is used to run a business. It is calculated by dividing the company's total liabilities – what it owes others, in the short term and long term – by the equity of the shareholders. Shareholders' equity is calculated as total assets minus total liabilities.

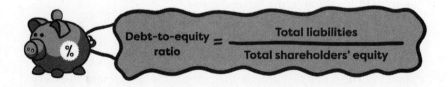

$$\text{Debt-to-equity ratio} = \frac{\text{Total liabilities}}{\text{Total shareholders' equity}}$$

As a potential investor in a company, you want this ratio to be neither too low nor too high. But each industry has different debt-to-equity ratio benchmarks, as some industries use more debt financing than others, so it can be tricky to work out the right level. Speaking in general terms, a fairly high ratio could signal a company is in financial distress. But one that's very low could be a sign the company is over-relying on equity, which can be costly and inefficient. In general, the lower the debt-to-equity ratio the better, as that indicates the company has taken on less debt.

A debt ratio of 0.5 means that there are half as many liabilities as equity. In other words, the assets of the company are funded 2 to 1 by investors to creditors. This means that investors own 66.6 cents of every dollar of company assets while creditors only own 33.3 cents on the dollar.

INVESTORS OWN TWO THIRDS (66.6 CENTS),
CREDITORS OWN ONE THIRD (33.3 CENTS)

Let's say a company has $100,000 of bank lines of credit, and a $500,000 mortgage on its property. The shareholders of the company have invested $1.2 million. The debt to equity ratio calculation would look like this:

$$\frac{\$100,000 + \$500,000}{\$1,200,000} = 0.5$$

If a debt-to-equity ratio goes up over time, the perceived risk of a company not making its interest payments goes up. Banks use this information to help them decide whether to lend a business more money. As an investor, you can use the information to decide whether you want to invest in the company.

Interest coverage ratio

This is another ratio used to measure how well a company can pay interest due on outstanding debt. 'Coverage' refers to how many times over the company can cover its interest obligations with its currently available earnings. It is sometimes called the 'times interest earned' (TIE) ratio. It's calculated by dividing a company's earnings before interest and taxes (EBIT), by its interest expense during a given period.[29]

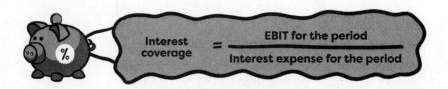

$$\text{Interest coverage} = \frac{\text{EBIT for the period}}{\text{Interest expense for the period}}$$

This ratio helps lenders, investors and creditors determine a company's riskiness relative to its current debt or future borrowing. If a company's current earnings far exceed the amount it needs to cover the interest payments on its debt, it has a buffer during possible future leaner times. On the other hand, if a company's current earnings don't allow it to comfortably meet its interest obligations, it may be in a more precarious financial position as it wouldn't take much of a dip in revenue for the company to experience financial issues.

Staying above water when it comes to interest payments is always a critical concern for a company. It's a red flag as soon as a business begins struggling with its obligations, because it may have to borrow further or dip into cash reserves to keep up to date.

So, what should you be looking for here as a potential investor? An interest coverage ratio of less than one signals poor financial health. Generally, three or above is regarded as the preferred amount for a company with solid, consistent revenues.

Fundamental analysis of share markets versus technical analysis

There are two major schools of thought about how to draw conclusions about the viability of a share: 'fundamental' analysis and 'technical' analysis.

They exist at opposite ends of the spectrum, like the cheer squads for two competing football teams. Investors and share traders alike use them both to make decisions about whether to invest in a share, or not, and when they're researching or predicting share prices. Just like every other investment strategy, both have pros and cons, and fans and detractors.

Fundamental analysis is a method of determining a share's real or 'fair market' value.[30]

Fundamental analysts study a range of factors that can affect a share's value, including the state of the economy, industry and market conditions, and how financially strong and well-managed individual companies are. Fundamental analysis assesses a range of things, including earnings, expenses, assets and liabilities – all the fun things on a company's balance sheet that we looked at earlier in the chapter.

The outcome of fundamental analysis is a score you can use as a point of comparison against a company's current market price, to assess whether the share is priced accurately (fair), has been overvalued (not ideal) or undervalued (money win!).

Technical analysis is where an investor attempts to identify opportunities in the market by looking at statistical trends, such as movement in the price and volume of shares. The base assumption of technical analysts is that all known fundamentals are factored into the share price, therefore there is no need to pay close attention to it. So they don't always love fundamental analysis, because they don't believe in measuring the intrinsic value of an asset. They prefer to look at share charts to see patterns and trends as a means of predicting future trends. For example, a fundamental analyst looking at Tesla shares would be diving into the company's assets, debts, liabilities, earnings and expenses to see how financially viable the company is. A technical analyst would be examining the trends of a market and its desire for that particular Tesla share.

QUANTITATIVE VERSUS QUALITATIVE DATA

Quantitative data is annual reports, numbers, statistics – the facts. It is about what is written on paper and what is drawn from facts and figures: the costs, the profits and the percentages. If it's in the annual report and it can be confirmed by a process of fact-checking, it's likely to be quantitative data.

Qualitative data is more subjective. You can't really argue with a statement like 'We made a profit of a million dollars last year,' but there's a lot more interpretation and flexibility when it comes to predictions – what might happen or is happening internally. Qualitative data includes things like the experiences of staff who have worked for that company, or of clients who buy their product.

WHAT HAPPENS NEXT?

You'll notice I haven't covered the ins-and-outs of how to actually purchase shares directly in a specific company within this chapter. That's because I really want to focus on helping you feel informed and empowered *first*, before you take any action.

The next step I'd recommend is to try your hand at some virtual trading, to get a taste of what it's like. Twice a year, the ASX Sharemarket Game opens and you can participate as an individual or in a group, investing virtual cash to see how it performs over 15 weeks based on your chosen test strategies.[31] You can even win prizes! It's a great way to get more comfortable with the process.

Phew, that was a *lot* of info, and probably some of it seems quite dense. But you know what they say – the bigger the challenge, the better the rewards (or something along those lines!). I think it's good to know the possibilities, even if you decide they're things for Future You to explore further. Remember, you can always seek professional financial advice if you want to ask lots of questions about direct investing, and for support and peace of mind.

Ultimately, information is power and if this is something that lights you up (like I know it does for me), for sure get out there and do the research that's going to help you grow your portfolio in this way! I believe in you, and your ability to play and succeed in this space.

● ● ● ● ● ●

DEONIE, 29 – ACT

Around 2019, before my husband and I were married, he told me about his plan to start buying shares. I was very sceptical because I didn't understand the process. My parents didn't invest in shares and so I knew nothing about it. After we got engaged in 2020, and he showed me his investing platform and tried to teach me about it, I felt comfortable enough to contribute some of my savings (which I had a lot of and wasn't doing anything with) to a fund. He wanted me to choose where my money went so I tried to think of something that might be affected by the pandemic, but would be likely to bounce back afterwards. I chose a travel business. He did the research and chose one that historically had paid good dividends, meaning it could potentially be a good long-term investment or shorter term if we wanted to cash out.

I was recommended SOTM just a few months ago and have worked my way through the podcast from the start: now I'm the one who instigated us having a dedicated 'investment' account in our bank and we have a portfolio worth almost $20,000. Our portfolio is a priority for us and although we have a large deposit ready for a house, we are questioning whether it's what we want for ourselves at the moment. We are aiming to get a passive income generated through our portfolio as soon as possible.

● ● ● ● ● ●

TAKE NOTE

If you're feeling confident and curious about starting
to invest in individual companies, definitely begin
by reading and understanding their annual reports
to help you assess their performance.

....

There are ratios that help potential investors to get a good read
on how well a company is doing; for example, its profitability
and solvency. Use these ratios in conjunction with each other.

....

Not quite ready to take this step yet? That's all good!
When you are ready, just remember to only take
financial advice from those qualified to give it.

....

Chapter 11

Investment strategies

What is an investment strategy and why do you need one?

Great question!

Let's talk about your investment strategy – what it is, why it's so important, and why I'd never recommend you invest without one.

We've covered a lot of ground together so far. Now, for you to be able to go and invest on your own, my goal is for you to understand some of the different types of investment strategies, all of which you might implement for different reasons.

Don't stress if 'investment strategy' sounds a bit full-on. When you come up with one, really you're just making a plan – and we make those all the time. I like to think of it as an outline that can help take you from where you are to where you want to be, and I think the best way to do this is to work backwards. (I'm a big fan of working backwards on lots of financial things – it's a great trick.)

Everyone wants to make money out of their investments, of course. We're here to build some wealth! But let's stop and really think for a minute: what is your overall, big-picture goal with investing? This is not *how much* money you want to have or create; it's the *why* do you want to have lots of money in the first place? Obviously, we all want to be comfortable and maybe even filthy rich, but what's driving that aspiration? What does that actually buy us?

Is your greatest wish to build financial security for your future, to take care of yourself (and any loved ones) in retirement, free from worry? Do you drift off to sleep thinking about building up serious seven-figure wealth so you can live the bougie life you've always dreamed of, complete with business-class holidays to Europe every winter, a luxe wardrobe and an upgrade in designer car every three years? Are you super keen to find ways to supplement your income so you can work less and live off the profits of your investments every month, so you can spend more of your time doing other things that really light you up?

Your answer to this 'why?' is *so* important because it will help you determine exactly which investment strategy suits you best, since once you have an idea of where you want to go with your investments, you can start taking action towards actually making it happen. Which is what I'm here to help with!

Funnily, though, this is the part that most people get back-to-front. I hear it all the time. They start investing in a certain stock or asset class because it seems like a good idea, their friend made a pretty penny off it, or they've seen media headlines saying that it's the hot ticket to wealth. Then, only once they've invested a small (or significant!) amount of money, do they start to think about their goals and what they're truly trying to achieve.

If your goal is too broad or vague – something like, 'I want to invest and make a profit' – then it's going to be really tricky trying to work out what to invest in and for how long, because your metric for success is so open-ended. We need a bit more to work with.

It's kind of like going to the hairdresser and saying, 'I'd like to walk out of here with my hair looking amazing.' No kidding! Of course you do! But do you want to achieve that outcome with a new cut? A fresh colour? Some balayage, a few foils to frame your face, or a fringe? The definition of good hair is different for everybody. You can't quantitatively assess 'looking amazing', and no matter how skilled they are your hairdresser will have a hard time providing you with the outcome you want if you're vague with your ask.

This is why we need to be specific in our goals. We need to have a clear direction and markers for our investing journey. We don't want to walk in asking for a trim and leave with a pixie cut! In the same way, we don't want to invest for yield, only to realise what we actually want is long-term capital growth.

● ●

GET SPECIFIC ON YOUR INVESTMENT GOAL

My overall goal with investing is:

....

● ●

There are plenty of ways to build wealth as an investor, and with different investment strategies you need to take into consideration a number of things like:

● your risk tolerance;
● your life stage;
● how much money you plan to invest;
● current market conditions.

Also keep in mind that your strategy will evolve over time because so will your life. You might not (and in fact, probably won't) have the same investment strategy forever.

There are four main strategies that arguably could suit different types of investors, regardless of what asset class or specific instrument you use. Whether it's direct investing, ETFs, managed funds, or property, choosing which type of investing strategy suits you best is the first move.

So, with your end goal in mind, I'm now going to run through these key strategies and how they work.

A little reminder before we dig in:

- **active** refers to investments that require your input and attention to generate a profit;
- **passive** refers to investments where you can be a little more hands-off.

DON'T SET-AND-FORGET

When you create an investment strategy, you're creating some rules or criteria that help you to make investing decisions. It's always about being strategic (the clue's in the name!).

Think of your investments like a garden. One part of the garden might be getting all of the water from the sprinkler, so we need to move it around, and water some of the other shrubs and flowers (in other words, pay attention to other investment classes).

Sometimes when we check in with our investment plan, we might decide everything is flourishing beautifully and we don't need to make any tweaks. How good! Other times, we might decide we need to replant our seeds, because even though the tomatoes did really well last season, we need to plant them in a different location for the next season to grow even *more* tomatoes.

My point? Deciding on a strategy is important, but checking in on it regularly is absolutely crucial. You'll be helping Future You big time by performing these frequent health checks!

Strategy 1: Value investing

Type: Active

Okay, let's get into it. The first investment strategy is value-based investing.

This is not to be confused with values-based investing, which is making decisions according to your values and ethics (something I'm a big believer in), as we discussed back in Chapter 8. What I'm talking about here is investing in something because you believe it's worth more than it's currently selling for.

Value-based investing can be quite uncertain, because you're making assumptions that something is undervalued. That might not actually be the case, but when you buy an asset under this strategy, you're following the old adage that I'm sure you've heard of buy low and sell high.

If you're adopting a value investing strategy, you're looking for something that's undervalued. What kind of thing could this be? An example might be an unrenovated property that needs just a few cosmetic touches to boost its value. In the share market, this could mean you have an inkling that a particular company's shares are being sold for a price that is much lower than what you think the company is worth.

How it works in practice is something like this. Say you're investing in shares, and you've been tracking a particular company, Super Fantastic Company A. After doing your research, looking at the documents and resources outlined in Chapter 10, you believe SFCA shares should be valued at around $25 each.

One day, the market presents an opportunity for you to purchase SFCA shares at a lower price than they have been trading at, or lower than you'd expect them to be valued at. In fact, they're just $19. Love it!

So you buy some of the shares, tuck them away in your portfolio and hold them over the long term (unless the need arises for you to rebalance your portfolio – more on that in Chapter 12).

Hot tip: There's the ability on a lot of share trading platforms for you to put a marker on an individual share, and then automatically purchase it if it drops to a certain level. Your automatic marker has been set up to buy when the share drops below, say $20, so your purchase gets triggered then. Great for busy women – and thanks to the power of automation you can literally purchase shares while you sleep!

A great example of this type of investing strategy in action is Warren Buffett's. He's the OG value investor – the guy that everybody in the industry looks at, because he's regularly able to pick (and buy) a stock that's undervalued. He does a TON of research on these things. Sometimes, it quite literally takes him years to make a decision on whether to buy. The total opposite of an impulse purchase!

You don't need to be a billionaire or a finance nerd to be a value investor. You don't need to read articles, annual reports and financial statements every day. But what you *do* need to have are some time, energy and solid research.

I want to point out here that there's a degree of irrationality in this strategy, because the market is incredibly smart and knows what's going on. There's usually a reason for a particular share price. So if you want to be a value investor, you're essentially saying that you've done your research and decided that you know better than what the market is saying.

I'm not saying it can't be done; I am saying it requires effort, energy, knowledge and perfect timing.

A NOTE ON SPECULATIVE SHARES

An investor looking at an **undervalued share** is trying to find a share that has been assessed or valued as being worth less than what it should be. Undervalued share traders are aiming to purchase shares 'on sale' to buy and hold long-term, in the hope that the market will eventually reflect their true value.

A **speculative share**, on the other hand, is a share that carries a really high level of risk, with the possibility of a really high rate of return. Speculative investing is purchasing a share that carries a lot of risk, and that risk is reflected in its price.

Speculative trading is often likened to gambling. Despite the market and information suggesting otherwise, the purchaser is hoping that their guesswork will ultimately pay off. That potential for a financial windfall is the compensation you *may* get in exchange for the risk.

In my view, investing in these shares is not a strategy, because it might be a winner, but it also might go to crap. You might end up with absolutely *nothing*. Not ideal!

If this is something you want to pursue, it's a good idea to look at the annual reports of the companies you're interested in and dig deep into the details. As mentioned in Chapter 10, the information in a report can help you make an informed investing decision. For instance, the company might show signs of financial weakness, or financial strength. It might not have a super sustainable business model, or it could show promising signs of growth for the future. It could be led by a switched-on CEO who has created other mega-successful businesses, and you might think the future looks bright. Or it could have an unproven leadership team who have next to no track record of scaling a business up to be a huge success.

Information is your friend here. Do the research. Make informed decisions.

As you know by now, I'm a big fan of taking as much emotion out of the investment journey as possible, and I strongly suggest you don't base your financial future on gut feelings. Instead, make sure you root your investment decisions in facts and figures. Promise you'll thank me later!

Strategy 2: Growth investing

Type: Active

Okay, on to strategy number two: growth investing!

These investors are chasing shares and assets that they believe have a significant upside when they hold the asset long-term. This could include an increase in the value of a company, or capital growth of a property asset.

These assets are on an upwards run, so they should be consistently growing. As a growth investor, you're essentially looking for the next Apple, or the next hot suburb or town: something that's really going to take off and *grow*. Many people look at the medical industry and science and technology for undervalued stocks, believing that their value may not have been seen yet in the marketplace. That said, this type of investing is not super speculative, because you're looking for a proven performer that still has a massive future ahead of it.

A fabulous example of this in recent years has been tech shares like Canva. Founded in Perth in 2013, Canva has had an epic growth run. In 2020, it was valued at around $6 billion. By 2021, that had grown to $15 billion. In 2022, Canva's market cap had quadrupled again to $60 billion. And many believe there's further growth in Canva's future, but who knows?

Canva is a privately held company, which means you weren't able to buy shares directly. At the time of writing, it is only accessible to large, institutional venture capital investors. An insto (as institutional funds are colloquially known in the investing world) is a pooled investment fund, only available to these large institutional investors, which is a rich company or organisation that invests money on behalf of other people. These funds build large portfolios for their clients with varying objectives, but they're usually companies, charities and governments. As an individual investor, you can buy into an institutional fund.

Unlike value investing, where you look at a company and think: 'Well, they're really underpriced,' in this case you're thinking, 'Wow, there's so much potential for them to grow.'

Ten years ago, for instance, Tesla might have fallen in this category. A lot of people who got on board at the Tesla IPO (initial public offering – the first time that shares of a private company are listed to the public to buy) would have been what we'd categorise as growth investors, because they saw the vision that Elon Musk believed he could pull off. They did the research and realised that Tesla was not just making electric vehicles, but it was also planning to make solar storage batteries.

So they took a punt, and that's paid off. In 2012, Tesla's share price was US$6.60. In 2022, at the time of writing, it's US$695.

Wouldn't we all like to find the next Tesla!

'So Victoria, what's the downside of this type of strategy? There must be one!'

Well, with growth investments, the upside is usually in the growth of the asset, and rarely in the ongoing yield or returns. For instance, most growth stocks don't generally pay dividends. The company's growing, so it's investing every dollar of profit back into its own growth. If you're a growth investor, you wouldn't want to be taking money out of the company while it's trying to expand and develop, because it needs as much as possible to keep growing.

The same principle applies with property. If you're investing in a growth property, it's likely that the rent you receive on it each week won't cover the full mortgage and ownership expenses. You may have to tip in $50, $100 or even a few hundred dollars a week to manage the investment.

Why would you want to *pay* money every week to hold an investment? Because, as a growth investor, you're playing the long game.

Consider a growth investor who paid $500,000 for a house in a sought-after Sydney suburb 20 years ago, and that same house is now worth $2 million. I'm betting they don't mind that they had to chip in some money here and there to cover the council rates or top up the mortgage over time, because they're sitting on seven figures of pure profit. Sounds pretty sweet to me.

Bottom line? You're likely to only make money from this stock if you sell it. Do you want to hold the asset long term and realise those profits down the track? Then growth investing could suit you.

But if you want profits and cash flow along the way, you may need to look at dividend stock. Let's check it out.

Strategy 3: Dividend investing

Type: Passive

Now we're moving into passive strategies and, as a reminder, the overall goal with these is to create wealth gradually over time. Some call these 'buy and hold' strategies – you are buying an asset with the intention to own it over the long term, not just to churn and burn. Unlike active investors, those who are passive investors aren't chasing gains from short-term price fluctuations or from trying to time the market.

Dividend investing is the yin to the yang of growth investing. As a dividend investor, you're someone who's prioritising buying shares that pay you an income. This is where you would look at blue chip, stable shares. They're an investment type that delivers profits immediately; you don't have to wait for growth or market conditions to change in order to get a financial benefit.

These types of shares consistently pay a solid dividend twice a year. Note that a dividend is your share of a profit of a business. If the company is not making profit (say, if it's had a not-so-profitable year or has chosen to reinvest profits for growth), you're unlikely to get a dividend. It's never guaranteed, but blue chip shares are the slow-and-steady steed that haven't let many people down before, which is why they're usually more expensive than other share types.

These are the proven performers, and if you're a dividend investor, then you're the type of person who favours stable, reliable and consistent returns, and you're willing to sacrifice huge amounts of growth in order to get it.

Take, for example, NAB shares. At the time of writing, NAB shares are valued at $30.81. Five years ago, in 2017, they were valued at $30.65. Five years before that, in 2012, they were valued at $22.21. And all the way back in 2002, two decades ago, they were worth $30.41.

There have been loads of peaks and troughs throughout that period – the share market is a rollercoaster and no shares are immune from the volatility. At different times, NAB's shares have dropped to $15 and soared to $40.

But a dividend investor isn't focused on that. They're not trying to buy the time for value, and they're not that fussed about the growth, either.

They're in it to get paid, y'all. Regularly.

When we look at NAB shares, the dividend paid has been consistent, if volatile. It has dropped as low as 10 cents and risen as high as 99 cents, but investors *always* got paid.

Typically, NAB announces a dividend with the release of its half-year results in May and full-year results in November, with dividends twice a year, in July (interim dividend) and December (final dividend). NAB has paid biannual dividends every year since 1982, including during the COVID-19 recessionary period.

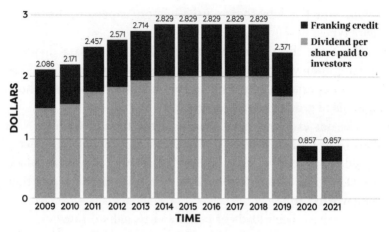

NAB share dividends 2009–2021

Strategy 4: Dollar cost averaging (DCA) investing

Type: Passive

The dollar cost averaging strategy is a strategy where you get to be a little bit less active, because you trust the market to do its thing.

The aim of DCA investing is to consistently invest over a long period of time. You're being consistent and putting money into the market on a regular basis. The investments you make could be growth, value or dividend options – or even a mix of all three. The specific type of investment strategy matters less than the action you're taking, which is essentially making use of the ebbs and the flows of the market to grow your exposure.

It works like this.

You decide on a specific amount you want to invest every month. Let's say $100.

You set up an automatic plan to purchase a specific share, ETF, managed fund or other type of asset in the amount of $100 a month, regardless of how much it is selling for. (Noting that fees, charges and/or commissions are likely to be payable on the purchase; remember to factor those in when doing your own calculations.) Sometimes the market is going to be up, and for each trade that you make, you end up with fewer shares than you might have purchased the month before. For instance, your $100 might get you two shares worth $50 each.

Sometimes there's a dip and you might end up with a whole heap more shares than you bought the month before. In our example below, when the share price drops to $10, $100 (excluding fees) would buy you ten shares.

This is a long-term strategy (ideally ten years minimum) and overall, you end up only ever paying the average price for that share. You'll buy at the peak and at the dip; most importantly, you'll keep buying.

Over the months and years, your holdings will grow and you'll eventually end up sitting on a profitable pot.

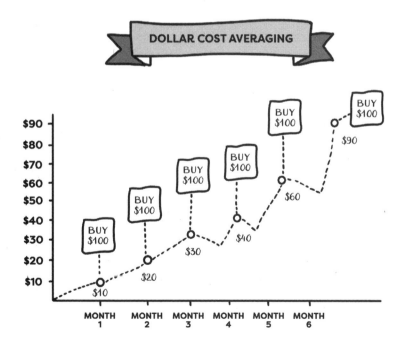

Dollar cost averaging versus single investment
(Source: Yahoo Finance (data), My Stock Market Basics blog)

This strategy is about being disciplined and investing consistently. It's quite powerful to automate your investing journey and to know that it's ticking away nicely, and you don't have to get too concerned about market conditions or following different trends and updates, because your passive strategy is to always be buying. You've got a plan and you're just getting on with it.

You can use this strategy to invest in an ETF, managed fund or individual shares, knowing that as long as you're consistent by continually investing in the market, the share price at the time doesn't actually matter to you. (Do be aware that it may heighten risk and reduce diversification if you're investing in only one particular share, though, as its price could drop for a serious reason.)

As somebody who has done all my research on the companies that I want to invest in personally and on behalf of my clients, and who spends five or six hours a week on Zoom calls with market specialists, I have a pretty good grasp of this investing stuff. And if I could use my education and expertise and connections to time the market and *always* buy in the dips, I would. But that's not realistic, for me or for the average, everyday investor.

That's why I think this is a really powerful strategy, because it means you get to put less labour in for a really good return. Dollar cost averaging also means that, although you'll most likely see the worst days of the market, you won't miss out on the best days.

As you can see from the table below, if you step out of the market and by doing so miss out on its best days of performance, that has the potential to chip away at your return. Not only is it tricky trying to time the market, it also carries risk!

4 January 1999 to 31 December 2018	Dollar value	Annualised Performance
Fully invested (S&P 500 index)	$29,845	5.62%
Missed 10 best days	$14,895	2.01%
Missed 20 best days	$9,359	-0.33%
Missed 30 best days	$6,213	-2.35%
Missed 40 best days	$4,241	-4.20%
Missed 50 best days	$2,985	-5.87%
Missed 60 best days	$2,144	-7.41%

The difficulties of trying to time the market (1)
(Source: JP Morgan)

The next table also helps to quantify how challenging it is to attempt to time the market. Panic-selling can mean missing the worst days – but also missing the best days, which often follow the biggest market drops. Instead, holding steady for a long period through the ups and downs – which in this example would have given a return of 17,715 per cent – may be the simplest recipe for reducing the likelihood of loss.

Decade	Price return	Excluding worst 10 days per decade	Excluding best 10 days per decade	Excluding best/worst 10 days per decade
1930	-42%	39%	-79%	-50%
1940	35%	136%	-14%	51%
1950	257%	425%	167%	293%
1960	54%	107%	14%	54%
1970	17%	59%	-20%	8%
1980	227%	572%	108%	328%
1990	316%	526%	186%	330%
2000	-24%	57%	-62%	-21%
2010	190%	351%	95%	203%
2020	18%	125%	-33%	27%
Since 1930	**17,715%**	**3,793,787%**	**28%**	**27,213%**

The difficulties of trying to time the market (2)
(Source: Bank of America, S&P 500 returns)

Just to be clear, this all assumes that the investment does increase over the long term, and that the investor (you!) is happy and able to stay invested during that time without needing to access the funds.

A mix of strategies = core satellite approach

Think of a planet, with all of its satellites orbiting around it.

This is the crux of a core satellite approach.

It means you have one main, core investing strategy – the planet – which is the investment strategy that makes the most sense for you overall.

Then you have satellites: they come and they go. Sometimes they're really big and can have a significant impact on the planet. Sometimes they slide on past without much fanfare. Sometimes they crash and burn. And that's totally okay! Because your satellites are not the main pillar of your investment strategy, you can afford to experiment a little.

The idea is that the core consists of passive investments while the smaller satellites are more actively managed and have a higher potential of earning greater returns.

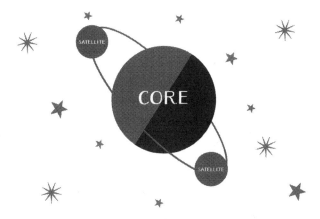

For example, your core strategy is DCA, but you also invest in a value stock from time to time. Or maybe you sink $500 into a growth stock, because it keeps you engaged in the investing world.

It's all about nourishing your needs and your interests while being mindful of what you want to achieve, without compromising the future financial security that you're building for yourself. If you have the chance to dabble in something that catches your eye but is a bit more experimental, while still pursuing your main plan, to me that sounds like a win–win scenario.

Now, I want to pause for a moment here to reiterate the importance of spending a decent chunk of time in the market. Check out the next two graphs – the first representing ten years of consistent investment, the second 30 years. Same initial deposit and monthly deposits for both – $500. On the second graph, look how much of the value at the end of the 30 years consists of the interest that's been earned. It's more than 70 per cent of the total! That, my friends, is time working its magic through the power of compounding. It doesn't bring immediate gratification, but imagine how you'd be feeling in year 30 if this was your portfolio!

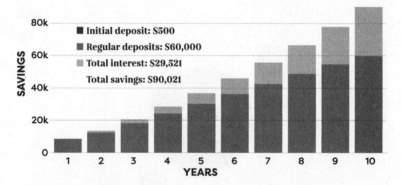

Investing $500 per month for 10 years with an initial deposit of $500. Compounding monthly, annual interest rate of 7.5%

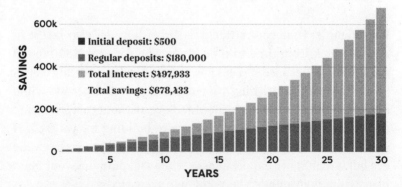

Investing $500 per month for 30 years with an initial deposit of $500. Compounding monthly, annual interest rate of 7.5%

Should I buy property or invest in shares?

I love receiving questions from the She's on the Money community, and there really are no bad ones, but I have to confess this is one of my most hated questions!

And the reason it's one of my most hated questions is because I can't answer it fairly – because I don't know your beliefs, I don't know your values, I don't know your income or what's accessible to you.

There's no right or wrong, generally speaking, but there might be a right or wrong *for you*, depending on all those things. It's such a personal journey.

If you're comparing an investment property with shares, I think it's not actually about return; it's about accessibility. The hurdles you may have to jump through in order to get into property are far higher than the hurdles to get into investing in shares.

A better question to ask in my view is: what do you want to achieve? Is it financial security or wealth? Is it a roof over your head? Is it an investment property that grows in value? Do you want to leave a legacy behind for future generations to thrive from? It's important to remember that even though the Australian dream is to own property, you can still build intergenerational wealth via other avenues.

When you're clear on what you want to achieve in your investing, you can sit down and work out the best way for you to achieve financial security. If you were my client, I'd ask questions like:

- What's your current living situation?
- Do you want to live in this location for the next five to ten years?
- What is the rental yield like in the area you're looking to purchase in?

- What's your income?
- What are your financial responsibilities?
- Do you have kids?
- Do you need to factor in childcare and private school costs?
- What are you trying to get out of your investments?
- What type of returns are you expecting from this asset class?

We'd use the answers to those questions to pick the asset class that makes the most sense for your goals. For some people, that answer is going to be property. For other people, it's not.

Keep in mind that wealth creation isn't about becoming a millionaire. It's about making money from investing and earning money *from* your money, so your employment is no longer your only source of income.

What I do know is this: in 2022, when buying a property is so unachievable for so many, wealth creation using other asset classes is possible for everybody, regardless of your income.

At the end of the day, the answer to this question is really personal. But hopefully by now, I've given you enough tools and resources to empower you to work towards answering this question for yourself.

Should I invest if I have a mortgage?

Another very common question! And I really get why you're asking. Again, it goes back to your values and goals, and what you want to achieve.

Let's say you pay off an extra $500 a month of your mortgage. What's that going to achieve? It will mean that you probably get out of the mortgage five years earlier, and then you can start investing in shares, right? That might be a really solid plan. Who doesn't want to pay off their mortgage debt and own their own home outright as soon as they can?

The alternative is that you don't contribute that extra $500 a month to your mortgage. Instead, you put it into the share market.

You pay your mortgage off over 30 years instead of 25 (and that will incur more interest paid on your mortgage). But what is your share portfolio going to be worth on the day that your mortgage finishes? Will you be in a better financial position long-term?

THE IMPACT OF $135,300

PAY OFF AN ADDITIONAL $500 PER
MONTH FROM A $600,000 LOAN
AT 3.5% INTEREST ON A 30 YEAR MORTGAGE

INVEST $500 PER
MONTH AT AN ASSUMED
RATE OF RETURN OF 7.5%
OVER 22.55 YEARS
(IDENTICAL PERIOD OF TIME
AS THE MORTGAGE REPAYMENTS)

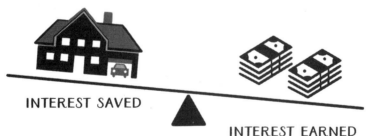

INTEREST SAVED

INTEREST EARNED

KNOCKING 7 YEARS AND
4 MONTHS OFF YOUR MORTGAGE
(BRINGING TOTAL MORTGAGE
PERIOD TO 22.55 YEARS)
TOTAL SAVING: $99,365

TOTAL INVESTED
$215,210.69
TOTAL INVESTMENT WORTH
$350,210.60
TOTAL RETURN: $134,999.91

This proposition changes if interest rates on mortgages are higher than the average rate of return. Then it may not be better to invest.

Mortgage interest rates at the time of writing are around 5 per cent. The average rate of return for the Australian share market over the last 30 years is 9.7 per cent.[32]

While I can't tell you what the 'right choice' is, as it's different for everyone, my hope is that these chapters are helping you work out which investment types resonate most with you.

In our final chapter, we'll join aaaaall the dots to help you come up with your own clear investing strategy. Bring it on!

In the meantime, the following reflection activity can help you clarify your goals and values.

● ●

WEIGH UP YOUR ASSET OPTIONS

Reasons I would want to buy property

Pros	Cons

Reasons I would want to invest in shares

Pros	Cons

Reasons I would invest in . . . (insert another asset you're considering!)

Pros	Cons

COURTNEY, 34 – NSW

I don't think I have a strategy, I'm really flying by the seat of my pants as I navigate being a baby investor. I need to spend more time learning about what types of strategies are out there and how to apply them. I have a lot more growing to do in the investment space but I feel like SOTM has been holding my hand, making me feel comfortable and guiding me in the right direction.

TARA, 37 – WA

I have been consuming a lot of information and talking with my husband. We are committed to getting a good strategy as we have got the house now and are ready for the next chapter. I am also 37, so it's time to do this. But I do think I might need professional advice because no matter how much I learn, I don't fully trust that I know enough to put myself and my husband in the best position long-term. But I am not wasting money, so I guess that is my current strategy!

LAURA, 29 – ACT

I have created an investment strategy for myself with specific short- and long-term goals in mind. I would like to explore this further though with my financial adviser to ensure my money is working in the most efficient way for me. My strategy includes my super, too. For a long time I was just with the super fund I got with my first job at 16. During COVID, I swapped jobs and was able to join an industry-specific super fund. I did extensive research before making the switch and I was impressed with how helpful their team was. I was excited to join a fund that does not invest in fossil fuels and has such a customer-centric focus. I've been able to choose an investment strategy that aligns with both my risk profile and personal values.

• • • • • •

TAKE NOTE

Understand the value of dollar cost averaging and know that nobody can time the market, because we don't have a crystal ball!

....

You hopefully now know which investment strategy aligns closest to your goals, values and risk appetite.

....

Recognise the power of time in the market. It's much more powerful than timing the market.

....

Chapter 12

Making tax less taxing

Many people don't love paying tax.

It's a constant theme that pops up in the message boards and DMs I receive from the She's on the Money community: people would much rather not be taxed. They'll do everything they can to avoid paying it! Some even go as far as to say their income has been 'swiped by the taxman'.

Time for a quick reality check, friends: that money was *never yours*.

The fact is, tax always has and always will be a necessary evil when you earn money – and that includes any money that you earn from investments. Some people get up in arms about paying a whack of tax to the government, but many of these same people aren't even the slightest bit concerned about how much they're wasting on extra fees to run two superannuation accounts!

As you've probably gathered by now, I have a totally different point of view than these people when it comes to tax. In fact,

I wrote a whole chapter about tax in general in my first book: why we pay it, what it's about, how to manage your tax obligations and more.

This time, I'm going to explore tax and what it means for you as an investor to try and make it all as straightforward as possible for you. I wouldn't say it's a pleasure to pay tax, but it's definitely a privilege – because if you're paying a lot of tax, that means you're making a lot of money!

Not to mention the pesky little fact that the taxes we pay help to fund everything from education, health care and infrastructure, and a million other important things we rely on to keep the Australian community ticking over. I'm sure, like me, you're grateful that those things exist to support our lives.

Taxes exist to benefit society as a whole. That's why I find the attitude of, 'I shouldn't have to pay tax' pretty toxic. We live in a society that has enabled us to grow a business to thrive, and I think it's only fair to repay the favour.

But back to my point!

I think tax is *really* sexy. By the end of this chapter, I hope you agree with me – and feel more comfortable about managing the process for your investments.

Tax considerations when you invest

'But Victoria, I've barely earned anything so far on my investments. Why do I need to bother with tax advice for such a minimal amount? I'm hardly a millionaire – yet!'

If you're investing small amounts of money at the beginning, you might think it's not all that important to get advice on the tax obligations for your investments. And I'm not going to pretend that tax advice is cheap; I hear you, and I know it's not necessarily affordable to everyone.

However, what you're paying for is expertise and advice in the current time, to set you up for the future. An accountant can also help you with forecasting and strategy, when you're calculating any returns that you hope to get on any form of investment. If you're in your first (tax) year of investing, when it comes time to do your tax return, you'll need to remember to factor in your investments – all things an accountant can help with.

As your investments grow and your exposure gets bigger, you could actually end up shooting yourself in the foot and costing yourself triple what the professional advice fees would have cost you (or even more!), because you didn't start thinking about the tax side of things early on.

I don't say this to scare you, but when it comes to tax, it's possible to end up in a pickle that can be really, really expensive to get out of. One really common way this happens is when people purchase a property in a specific name. If you buy an investment property, do you buy it in your own name? Do you buy it in joint names with your partner? What if one of you earns a ton more than the other? Do you set up a trust and buy it in that name?

Each of these options comes with different tax obligations and benefits. Depending on your unique situation, the right answer could be any of these. That's why it pays to get the right advice upfront – as it's too late to make these kinds of decisions *after* you've bought the property.

Another example of this is how you structure the debt on an investment property. I have a friend who bought an investment property a few years back – and he paid all cash. He still has a huge mortgage on his own home, but he decided to put down $400,000 in cash for the investment property.

I haven't had the heart to tell him that he's missed out on literally tens of thousands of dollars in tax deductions because of this decision. If he'd put that $400,000 on his own (non-tax deductible) home mortgage, and taken out a full mortgage against the investment property, every dollar he spent in mortgage interest on the investment property would have been a tax deduction.

Instead, he's receiving a solid weekly rent – and paying almost half of it in tax, all because he didn't structure his debt correctly at the beginning.

Another bonus is that the right tax advice can help you optimally manage your share investments, too, when it comes to timing the purchase and sale of shares to minimise your capital gains tax. I'll dig into CGT more in a moment, but first, I want to acknowledge that this topic doesn't come easily to everyone.

Some of you are probably itching to skip past this chapter already. Maybe you haven't even done your tax for the last year or two (or longer – eek!) and the whole thing stresses you out so you want to move on to the next chapter, pronto.

Or you might realise that perhaps you haven't done things in the right order in the past. Maybe, like my friend, you've made big financial decisions without getting the right advice, and now you're paying the price.

Please don't beat yourself up if any of this sounds like you. But remember, burying your head in the sand is *not* the answer to creating wealth. If you picked up this book, then you're here to get educated and sometimes you need to feel a bit uncomfortable to move through, grow and change to put yourself in the best possible position.

Making a mistake doesn't make you less smart; it just means that you made a decision, and it turned out not to have been the right one at the time. You used the tools and resources you had at the time, and now you have different ones because you're making the effort to get them, which means you can change the outcome next time.

You don't want to be stuck with that poor-performing asset or that bad structure that's not helping you move forward. Often this happens because your ego is too caught up in the decision you made.

This is really, really common – way more common than you might think!

But if you have made a mistake – say you've invested in the wrong name or in a less tax-effective entity, or purchased an asset without using debt, or you've bought an asset that is going backwards and you're not sure how to get out of it – then rest assured we've all been there. It happens to everyone. It's how we learn.

Later I'll touch on how to rebalance a portfolio or move your position forward if you're stuck in a bit of a 'situation'. But first, let's run through some of the most common tax terms and jargon, so we're all on the same page.

> You wouldn't get advice on buying diamonds from a bricklayer. So when it comes to tax, don't ask your mates for advice.
>
> Ask someone who is actually educated in how to help you structure your assets and investments to minimise the amount of tax you pay. You can even claim your accountant's fees at tax time, winning!

Tax terms

Capital gain

If you buy an asset or investment and then sell it for *more* than the cost to acquire it, you make a capital gain. You need to include all capital gains in your tax return in the financial year you sell the investment. Now, the whole process is far more complex than those two sentences might make it sound! And I don't have the space to get into all the nitty-gritty of different scenarios here, so for more detail that's relevant to you, I'd recommend having a chat with your accountant.

Capital loss

If you sell an investment for *less* than the cost to acquire it, you make a capital loss. You may be able to use this loss to offset the gain you've made on other investments in that financial year.

You can use a capital loss to reduce capital gains made in the year the loss occurs, or carry forward the loss to offset future capital gains. In general, as an individual you should be able to carry forward a tax loss indefinitely – there's currently no limit. However, you can't deduct a net capital loss from your personal taxable income; you can only apply it to capital gains you might make in future years. Sound confusing? Let's say that in FY2022–23, you sold one of your shares for a $10,000 loss. For this example, we'll assume it's a rough year for the share market so you don't have any capital gains you can apply that loss to. It can therefore be 'carried forward'.

Fast forward a year, we're in FY2023–24, let's say the market has picked up and you sold one of your shares for $50,000 profit (woohoo!). Your accountant should be able to deduct your previous tax loss of $10,000, reducing the capital gains you'll need to pay tax on. However, it's worth noting you must claim the deduction at the first opportunity you get (in other words, the first year that there is taxable income). If losses can be offset against the current year's income, then they need to be – so in that case, you can't choose to hold on to losses to offset them against future income.

Capital gains tax (CGT)

CGT is the tax you pay on your capital gains. For instance, if you buy a property for $500,000 and sell it two years later for $700,000 (nice work!), you would declare a capital gain of $200,000 in the tax year in which you sold the property. This may be lowered if you have allowable tax deductions and reductions to your cost base.

Although it is referred to as 'capital gains tax', a capital gain is considered part of your income rather than being a separate tax.

If you have a capital gain, it will increase the tax you need to pay, as it is likely to push you into a higher tax bracket. In the above example, the $200,000 gain is added to your income in the year the asset is sold, and you pay tax at the applied tax rate.

Hot tip: Under current tax law, if you are an individual Australian resident and own an asset for longer than 12 months, you're entitled to a 50 per cent discount on CGT.

Why? Because the government wants to encourage people to buy and hold long term, not churn-and-burn through their investments. This essentially means that of your $200,000 gain, $100,000 would be taxed.

According to the ATO, for complying super funds the discount is 33.33 per cent, and companies are not entitled to the discount.

Remember when I said it's super important to get the buying structure right at the beginning? Imagine if you bought an asset in a company name, thinking that was the best decision, only to discover that you don't have access to the 50 per cent CGT discount, and you have to pay way more tax than you would have if you'd bought it in your own name?

This is why getting the right advice is crucial! It pays for itself, and then some.

Negative gearing

Negative gearing is when you borrow money (such as a mortgage) to buy an income-producing asset (such as a property) that produces *less* income than is needed to pay for and maintain the asset in the short term. For instance, you buy an investment property that costs $800 a week to service, but the rental income is only $600. This asset is negatively geared by $200 a week, and you will need to make up this shortfall out of pocket. This gap amount can generally be claimed on your tax return.

Positive gearing

Positive gearing is when you borrow money (such as a mortgage) to buy an income-producing asset (such as a property) that produces *more* income than is needed to pay for and maintain the asset in the short term. For instance, you buy into a managed fund with a margin loan that costs $5,000 a year, but the dividends or returns are $10,000 a year. This asset is positively geared by $5,000 a year. This income must be declared on your tax return and will be taxed at your marginal tax rate.

How to rebalance a portfolio

Rebalancing a portfolio is like re-weighting the assets that you have. It usually involves buying or selling assets in a portfolio and then replacing them with other things that might create more diversification. A lot of people might start off with a balanced portfolio, but then over time, it changes.

Hot tip: Keep in mind that your investment portfolio isn't just what is on your investment report from your shares or stockbroker. It includes the cash in your personal bank accounts, assets that you own, and the crypto you dipped into because FOMO led you there.

I'm talking about rebalancing in this chapter because it can have tax implications, as buying and selling assets in order to rebalance can trigger a CGT event. So it's super important to establish (by speaking with your accountant) what the tax ramifications might be *before* you dive in and start reallocating things in your portfolio!

What rebalancing your portfolio does is help you stick to your original asset allocation strategy and also act upon any tweaks you decide to make to your investing style. No matter what's happening in the market, by rebalancing you're better able to stay true to your investing plan. It comes back to what I said before about how you don't want to just set and forget. Instead, regularly review and rebalance if you need to!

When you want to rebalance your portfolio, you absolutely could work this out for yourself, but, assuming you're not a fund manager or a finance expert, if you're planning on rebalancing an investment portfolio, then you should seek some advice for sure.

This is where the beauty of managed funds and ETFs lies, because the responsibility is on the fund manager or the ETF manager to make sure you always have a balanced portfolio. It can bring peace of mind to know that's being taken care of for you.

If you realise that how you've structured your investments so far is not resulting in the best outcome for you, I'd suggest you go see a tax professional who can help you with it.

It's also a matter of putting into practice everything you've read in this book so far:

- Get an understanding of your risk tolerance.
- Learn about the different investing strategies, and work out which one suits you best.
- Take stock of the investments you have and why they're not working for you.
- Look at the bigger picture, then make a decision to course-correct.

Overweight shares: You are too heavily invested in a particular share or asset class, so your portfolio is unbalanced and overweight.

Underweight shares: You don't have enough invested in a particular share or asset class, so your portfolio is unbalanced and underweight.

I do declare!

You have to declare all of your income that you earn from investments in your tax return. Let's say you invested $100 in the share market and it paid a dividend of $10.

You declare that 10 per cent income from those shares, and that income is then taxed at your marginal tax rate. Which might be 19 per cent, or 32.5 per cent, or 37 per cent, or 45 per cent. (In some cases, the income could push you into a higher tax bracket – as in the example below.)

This is the point where a lot of people get frustrated, because they don't allocate for that tax when investing. And it can feel like a bit of a slap in the face if it's unexpected. But you haven't actually been screwed here, so try not to think of it like that! In reality, it means that you ended up with more money, which means you pay a little more tax.

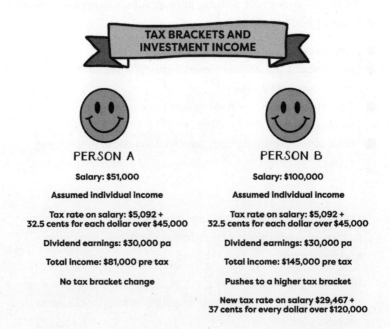

TAX BRACKETS AND INVESTMENT INCOME

PERSON A

Salary: $51,000

Assumed individual income

Tax rate on salary: $5,092 + 32.5 cents for each dollar over $45,000

Dividend earnings: $30,000 pa

Total income: $81,000 pre tax

No tax bracket change

PERSON B

Salary: $100,000

Assumed individual income

Tax rate on salary: $5,092 + 32.5 cents for each dollar over $45,000

Dividend earnings: $30,000 pa

Total income: $145,000 pre tax

Pushes to a higher tax bracket

New tax rate on salary $29,467 + 37 cents for every dollar over $120,000

Common tax mistakes and how to avoid them

When you're new to investing, there is *so* much to take in. While it is all incredibly exciting, I know it can also be a little daunting. So, to help ease the overwhelm, I've rounded up the common tax mistakes I see first-time investors making, so you can enjoy a seamless investing experience.

Not realising you'll need to pay tax on earnings/ dividends and not planning ahead

I've lost count of the number of times people have been shocked to discover at the end of June that they do, in fact, need to pay tax on their investment earnings. Just like any other kind of income, you're required to pay tax on your dividends and any capital gains.

To avoid getting stung at tax time, make sure you're aware of your tax obligations and set a little money aside at every paycheck to ensure they're covered.

Not reporting all of your income

If you're investing on multiple platforms or in multiple asset classes (e.g. rental income, crypto etc.) and don't report it, there's a very good chance the ATO will chase you down. They may even dish out a fine.

Sometimes when people invest in multiple ways or across multiple platforms, they can lose track of the money they have coming in and genuinely forget which income streams are coming from where. Unfortunately, the ATO won't just give you a pass for forgetting, so it's your responsibility (maybe with the help of an accountant) to ensure you're across all of your investments, so you can report your income accurately at tax time.

Forgetting to claim capital losses to offset capital gains

While we need to pay tax on any capital gains we make over the life of our investment, it's handy to know that any capital losses – any investment you sell for less than it was bought for – can be used to reduce capital gains made in the same year. Or alternatively you can hold on to the loss and offset any capital gains you make down the line. Sure, we may feel inclined to try and forget our less successful investment ventures, but it can actually pay to keep them front of mind to maximise other investments!

Buying and selling too quickly

As I've mentioned, when we sell our assets for more than we bought them for, we're required to pay a tax on that capital gain. If you sell your asset within the first 12 months of having bought it, then you'll need to pay tax on that entire gain at your regular marginal tax rate. This tends to happen particularly with crypto-currency purchases.

By contrast, if you hold on to your assets for a little longer (longer than 12 months), you'll get to make the most of the 50 per cent discount, which essentially halves the amount of tax you would pay otherwise. Moral of the story? Don't buy and sell too quickly!

Moving too slowly with an inheritance property

One of the common mistakes I see people make occurs when they inherit a property and sit on it for too long. I'd never want you to feel pressured to make an immediate decision about this sort of thing, as an inheritance is often wrapped up in a tidal wave of emotions which can cloud your judgement and influence your choices. However, it is important to be aware that if you inherit a property there may be tax implications that are time-bound, such as potential CGT exemptions, so it's a good idea to consult a tax professional.

Not keeping records well (a headache at tax time) and not holding on to them for long enough

We love an organised moment at She's on the Money and that's not just because we're obsessed with spreadsheets. When it comes to tax time, you won't be scrambling to retrieve a year's worth of information from all over the place.

'But Victoria, what exactly should I be keeping track of? Help!'

Make sure you hang on to important information like contracts of asset purchase or sale, and also be sure to make note of any income made from investments along the journey. Don't forget to document expenses accrued from services used to help manage your investments, like fees for a financial adviser. Once you've set up your system and have your documents organised, remember to hold on to them for a minimum of five years (noting that some documents have even longer holding periods), so if the ATO comes knocking and asks you to substantiate your claims, you're ready to go!

The common mistake when flipping shares

CGT is applicable if you own an asset such as a stock and you sell it and make a capital gain. As mentioned, if you own the asset for less than 12 months, you won't be eligible to get a discount on the capital gains you made on that asset. That's definitely worth considering in your investment strategy.

For instance, let's say someone buys $10,000 worth of shares, and then they sell them six months later for $15,000. At tax time, they have to declare that $5000 gain, and pay income tax on the full amount.

But if they held on to the shares for longer, and sold them 12 or 13 months later for $15,000, they should be entitled to the 50 per cent discount. When they declare the $5000 gain, only half of it is taxable.

Investing and your tax return

As we saw earlier, it's really important to keep good records of all of your investment actions and activities so you can properly account for everything at tax time (plus being organised with this stuff is a super sweet feeling).

The good news? Most platforms and apps should give you a statement or a summary that pulls together a record of your transactions through the year. They usually provide this in July, just after the end of the financial year, and you can use these statements to help you:

- Keep track of the different investments you own.
- Keep track of the costs of buying and selling the investments (i.e. cost base).
- Report any investment income.
- Claim the tax deductions you're entitled to.
- Calculate any capital gains or losses when you sell an investment.

For all investments, including shares, ETFs, managed funds, property and cryptocurrencies, you need to keep records that show:

- How much you paid for it: things like contracts for purchase of the asset and receipts.
- How much you sold it for: if you sold it. The date is important, as owning an asset longer than 12 months triggers the 50 per cent CGT discount.
- Any income you get from the investment: such as dividends or rental yields. Keep all records of income such as statements and receipts.
- Expenses incurred while owning the investment: such as tax invoices and receipts for payments made to manage, maintain or improve the investment.

Generally, you should keep tax records for five years after the date you included the income and/or capital gain or loss in your tax return.

So that's tax! I hope you're now feeling much clearer on how to factor it into your investing journey, you know what to do when tax time next rolls around and you've forgiven yourself any blips you might've had in the past.

With that ticked off, let's move ahead to the exciting stage of forming your investment plan!

• • • • • •

ABBY, 30 – WA

My parents never really talked about money. My husband's parents had a difficult money journey and though they were earning a lot and owning a business, they ended up in lots of debt and declaring bankruptcy, eventually selling their family home to downsize and pay down debt. They still live pay to pay and have the 'best of everything' – this has made us want to have something to show for how hard we work when we are older. We have $5000 invested in shares, mostly invested this year. We took a little while to settle on a platform we liked and so we did a bit of moving around. I'm a bit anxious about tax time!

ALLISON, 30 – NSW

After my separation, my ex and I rented our home to a tenant for a while. I didn't enjoy being a landlord, but the tax benefits that came from negative gearing weren't bad! In the year my ex and I rented out our house, we claimed a loss which meant I got about $1000 tax back that I wouldn't have had otherwise. We were lucky enough to sell our house at the top of the market. Frustratingly, I now can't get back into the property market as a single woman, despite the killer deposit I walked away from the sale with.

• • • • • •

TAKE NOTE

Don't forget to account for the fact that you will need
to be paying tax on any dividends or rental income you
receive or you'll be in for a nasty surprise at tax time!

....

While you might feel like investing is set-and-forget, always
being aware of your portfolio is super important. Ideally, aim
to review and potentially rebalance your portfolio annually.

....

You can avoid having to pay 50 per cent of your CGT by
holding your assets for a minimum of 12 months.

....

Chapter 13

Your investment plan

Okay, we've talked the talk, now it's time for you to walk the walk!

Hopefully by now you have a strong understanding of why you want to invest and what goals you're working towards. You know your money personality and risk appetite, and with your new understanding of the different asset classes and investment strategies, it's time to put together an official plan.

Before you get started, it is *so* important to make sure you're financially in a position where investing is a viable option. It will mean you can really get going with confidence. Run through this checklist to see if you tick all the boxes:

- I have money set aside for emergencies.
- I'm on top of my bad debt (more on this in a couple of pages), and investing isn't going to impact this.
- I fully understand my personal spending habits and have allocated money for investing in my cash flow plan.

● I have a basic understanding of shares, bonds, ETFs and index funds.

● I'm ready to start putting Future Me first.

How to create a Personal Investment Plan

You didn't come this far to walk away without a real, tangible plan you can start implementing immediately . . . right?

Unfortunately, I can't just hand that to you on a silver platter, much as I would really love to. But I CAN help guide you through everything you need to do, to dot all your i's and cross all your t's when it comes to creating your very own plan that's tailored to you.

You won't be surprised to hear that I really want you to focus on your goals. Setting goals is so important, and helps you keep on track and measure your success. Unfortunately, simply setting a goal doesn't mean you'll achieve it – that's the hard part. But don't worry, I'm right here holding your hand to get it done.

Planning is a very big part of my job (I'm a financial *planner*, after all!) and it's about to become yours too. We're going to break down these big goals of yours into bite-sized pieces that you'll be able to work on day-to-day, so that you can achieve everything you want.

Before we get into the depths of this, I want to be clear: this is in no way, shape or form a substitute for personal financial advice from a qualified financial adviser. As much as I'd love to distil here everything I do when I create a financial plan with my clients, it's impossible. My Statements of Advice are more often than not 80+ pages, and in the many years I've been an adviser, I've never created two that were the same! Personal financial advice is just that: it's personal.

What I can do, though, is give you a step-by-step guide to creating a broad investment plan that will get your ball rolling.

When we think about our investment goals, they're very likely to be long-term. Goals like saving for retirement or investing for your children's futures don't (and can't!) happen overnight, which means we need a plan to keep us on track over the long term. Creating a personal investment plan is going to require all of the following eight steps:

1. Understand your current situation.
2. Solidify your financial goals.
3. List out the pros and cons.
4. Finalise your investor risk tolerance.
5. Choose what to invest in.
6. Choose where to invest.
7. Implement your investment plan.
8. Review and rebalance.

In moving forward with creating an investment plan, you're acknowledging that you're not in any significant consumer debt and you've already established an emergency fund.

So let's start putting together a plan, one that's perfectly fit for your situation – because you made it! In the following few pages, we are going to navigate the eight outlined steps above to create a plan.

1. Understand your current situation

Financial freedom looks different for everyone. Once you realise this, you can start working towards your own.

The basis of financial freedom comes down to two things: spending less than you're earning, and regularly and continuously saving and investing.

It's tempting to assume that the more money you earn, the more financially free and empowered you will be. This isn't necessarily the case, though. You could be making a quarter of a million a year but if you're splurging it unwisely, you're not going to be financially well-off. While more money certainly helps, I could give you several examples of people I know who have an abundance of income and/or wealth, but still feel like they're sinking in quicksand. They make more than $250,000 per year, but somehow still live pay cheque to pay cheque. With that in mind, you simply cannot say, 'When I make more money, things will be better.' More income will not always solve your problems; if you don't change the way you approach money, it will compound them.

On paper, it's quite simple. If you spend less than you earn and invest regularly and continuously over the long term, you are likely to build up a large investment base. The investment industry likes to make it seem more complex than it is, because that's how they make money. I'm the opposite – I like to make things as simple as possible.

So, if you haven't already, it's time to calculate how much you've got coming in, how much you've got going out and the amount left over – which are going to be your dollars for investing!

● ●

EARN, SPEND, OWN, OWE

What you'll need:

While you may know these figures off the top of your head, it is handy to have access to your bank account, payslips and/or credit card statement.

Write down four monthly numbers: earn, spend, own, owe.

Earn

This is any net income that comes into your bank account in a month that you can allocate to something. This may come from a salary, side hustle, investment or allowance. If you have a variable income, write down the lowest amount you would earn on average.

If any extra comes in, this can be considered a surplus and be allocated to savings or investments later on.

Spend

This is any money that goes out of your bank account in a month. From rent to food to fun to bills to bank fees, calculate the total money leaving your possession in a single month. It's okay if this is an average, as this will fluctuate from month to month.

Own

What you own is really important to figure out. I'm not talking about whether you have a nice car, because I don't classify that as a wealth investment. I'm asking how much money you have in your superannuation account. Do you own a home yet? What assets do you have? A property? A savings account? I'm talking here about anything that could be sold for monetary value or that produces an income.

Owe

Do you have any debt? For instance, a personal loan, HECS-HELP, credit card debt or a mortgage? It's important to note that not all debt is created equal. Good debt, like an investment property loan, helps you to build wealth or increases your prospects to build wealth, thereby enhancing your life. In contrast, bad debt costs you money without improving your financial position. It involves borrowing money to purchase rapidly depreciating assets or only for the purpose of consumption. Examples of bad debt include money you borrow through credit cards and personal loans to pay for day-to-day expenses, holidays or an asset – such as a car – that tends to decrease in value. Just like the loans I had in my early twenties that I told you about in Chapter 1. (There's also okay debt, which doesn't necessarily return a monetary income you can see, but doesn't terribly affect cash flow either.)

Earn ....

Spend ....

Own ....

Owe ....

Okay, now that you have your four numbers, how do they look?

If you deduct what you owe from what you own, that will give you your net worth. If you deduct what you spend from what you earn, that will show you how much cash flow surplus or deficit you have each month. That surplus – if you're in a position where you have one – is what you have to potentially invest with!

Total assets (own) – total liabilities (owe) = ...

Total income (earn) – total expenses (spend) = ...

Available surplus for investing = ...

● ●

2. Solidify your investing goals

Now we know exactly where you're standing, we need to look at your goals and turn them into plans. You've heard it from me before and you're going to hear it from me again right now: I believe we *can* achieve everything – just not all at once.

Goal setting for me is a little bit like a process of elimination. It's nice to be open and optimistic about it at the beginning and to see how big you can dream. In my first book, I encouraged you to write down ALL your dreams, no matter how wild (and if you haven't done that activity yet, I really do encourage you to go back and try it!).

While I don't want you to forget any of those dreams, now is the time to be really clear and pull out your investment goals so we can get to working on those specifically.

This gives you some solid financial goals to start working towards, which you can then reverse-engineer. Don't roll your eyes if 'working backwards' makes you think of Year 9 algebra! I promise this is the kind of working backwards you'll actually use.

The reason I suggest you work backwards is because it prompts you to think about – and calculate – what your investment portfolio could look like in, say, 40 years, based on what you're starting with today. This brings it all to life and for me personally, plugging in the numbers and seeing what comes out the other side puts a massive smile on my dial, as it reminds me about the power of investing.

The Moneysmart compound interest calculator is a powerful (and free!) tool that can help you work out how much you might want to invest over a certain period of time. It allows you to input your initial deposit, your regular deposit, your deposit frequencies (daily, weekly, fortnightly, monthly, annually), and then you select your desired time frame. You then edit the interest rate, or the expected rate of return.

You can play around with the figures to see the potential impacts that regular contributions and compound interest or investment returns can amount to. Can you see now why I'm such a big fan of working backwards? When you want to achieve a long-term goal, this puts you in the driver's seat and makes the process not only easier, but far clearer.

Here's what you're going to need to work backwards on your goals:

Your goal

This is what you're planning to achieve, your end investment goal. It's where you'd consider your goal achieved. If your goal is to retire with a $60,000 income stream, then this is when you would have achieved that. If your goal is to save $50,000 for a house deposit, then this is your goal.

Keep in mind the SOTM model of setting goals.

Specific

The more specific the goal, the better. Knowing an exact amount needed and a deadline for completion will keep you focused, motivated and on track. For example: 'I will save $5000 to put towards share investments by 1 December' or 'I will double my credit card's minimum repayment every month until it is paid off'.

Optimistic

If your goals don't match your values, it'll be mighty hard to stick to them. And while I want you to be realistic, I also want you to be optimistic. You might think you can't break old spending habits or ever earn enough to invest in shares or property, but I'm here to tell you that you can.

If you need someone to give you permission to be financially independent, I will be that person!

Time-bound

Put a date on it and work backwards. Let's say you want to achieve financial freedom by retirement and you're currently 20 years old. You want an investment portfolio worth around $1.5 million by the time you retire at age 65. In this scenario you can work backwards to establish that you'd need to set and stick to a goal of investing $500 per month, starting with a deposit of $500 and assuming an annual interest rate of 7.5 per cent.

Measurable

Creating goals that you can quantify will keep you accountable. For example, you want to save $40,000 for a house deposit and have given yourself 36 months to achieve this. Break down the numbers. If you want to have $40,000 in a savings account in three years, you will need to save roughly $1112 a month, or you can break it down weekly. Give yourself numbers you can actively measure and work with. That way, if you don't meet your savings goal at an intended milestone, you can identify it immediately. Take pause to look at your bank statements or your budgeting/spending spreadsheet. Notice where you didn't hit your target and continue with that goal, but adjust your behaviour. Alternatively, you can adjust the goal to something more realistic and achievable. This is fine too, so long as you are still making progress and feeling positive about your goals!

Take a look at the table on the next page and try to fill it in as thoroughly as possible. Doing so can help you pin down your goals and stay on target!

Your starting point

Today! All great journeys start with a single step, and now is the time to take yours. This could be having no investment income at all, it could be $100 or even $1,000,000. All we need is to be clear about what our starting point is.

Your method

This is how you're planning to achieve this goal. Everyone's method is going to be different, but this is where the SOTM framework comes into play because, as we all know, the easiest way to fall off track or become disenchanted with the process completely is to set an unrealistic goal for yourself.

First, work out what return you'd like from your investment. For example, say you want to retire with an income stream of $60,000, on page 241 are some calculations based on that, and other, income streams.

RECAP YOUR GOALS

Priority	Goal	Total Cost	Term Short = 1 year Medium = 2–10 years Long = 10+ years	Duration	Monthly Cost	Target Date

YOUR CALCULATIONS

To work out how much money you need in your portfolio to achieve for example, a 5 per cent income stream, we take our goal income stream and times it by 20 (as 20 x 5 = 100 per cent).

$60,000 income stream × 20 =
$1,200,000 investment portfolio required

$80,000 income stream × 20 =
$1,600,000 investment portfolio required

$100,000 income stream × 20 =
$2,000,000 investment portfolio required

Hot tip: These are broad, basic calculations that don't factor in income tax (nor inflation). You will need to take that into consideration for a more detailed calculation – I can't do it for you as I don't know your tax rate!

$_____ × 20 = $_____
        income stream   investment portfolio required

Now we have taken our income goal and worked out what the real goal is, we have to take into consideration the time we have to achieve this goal.

You might find that there is a bit of back and forth with this process, to work out what is *really* achievable for you.

Please don't be disheartened or throw your hands in the air if you break the goal down and it feels too overwhelming or unachievable! Instead, start tweaking things. Change the amount of time you're giving yourself, or the end goal, to something less scary and more achievable for you and your situation.

As a guide, assuming you start with $0 initial deposit and you're earning an interest rate of 5 per cent, here's what you need to save in order to hit a range of financial targets:

Monthly investment made	$100	$200	$500	$1000
Investing for 10 years	$15,528	$31,056	$77,641	$155,282
10 years adjusted for inflation	$13,617*	$27,234*	$68,086*	$136,172*
Investing for 20 years	$41,103	$82,207	$205,517	$411,034
20 years adjusted for inflation	$31,097*	$62,195*	$155,487*	$310,975*
Investing for 30 years	$83,226	$166,452	$416,129	$832,259
30 years adjusted for inflation	$53,537*	$107,074*	$267,684*	$535,368*
Investing for 40 years	$152,602	$305,204	$763,010	$1.53M
40 years adjusted for inflation	$82,342*	$164,684*	$411,709*	$823,419*
Investing for 50 years	$266,865	$533,730	$1.33M	$2.67M
50 years adjusted for inflation	$119,319*	$238,638*	$596,594*	$1.19M*

*Assumed 2.5% rate of inflation

It's important to take inflation into consideration. Inflation is an increase in price, but not value (sadly!) which means $1 today is not worth the same as it is tomorrow. Inflation lowers your purchasing power, and will lower the value of your investment.

If you've listened to my podcast, you'd know that I usually explain this using the good old Maccas cone. In 1991, a Maccas soft serve cone was 30c and is now up to $1. The value went up (to $1) but the real value of the cone is still there, it's just a Maccas cone, it's just going to cost you more today than it would have in 1991. We need to take that into consideration so that in the future we can still afford the lifestyle we have today, with the money we have then.

● ●

MY CALCULATIONS

My desired investment income (annual): ....

My time frame: ....

My initial deposit: ....

My monthly contributions: ....

My total contributions: ....

My future portfolio value: ....

For example, Sarah is 20 years old and earns $70,000 per annum plus superannuation. Sarah wants to create an income stream outside of her superannuation that will give her $40,000 of income per year from when she turns 60.

Sarah's desired investment income (annual): $40,000
Sarah's time frame: 40 years
Sarah's initial deposit: $1,000

Sarah's monthly contributions: $1,000

Sarah's total contributions: $480,000

Sarah's future portfolio value: $1,533,379 (adjusted for inflation)

Remember that you can use an online calculator tool that adjusts for inflation, as well as the table above, to help you out.

● ●

3. List the pros and cons

You're doing GREAT so far! Next, I'm going to ask you to think about the decisions you're making, and weigh them up to ensure you're confident they're the right ones. We need to give some very serious thought to our strategies, because whenever there is a choice being made, something else is going to be sacrificed. That's just the way the financial cookie crumbles.

You need to now look at the pros and the cons of each option. I want you to give this a crack for each of your goals. Compromise is important in any relationship, and it's especially important in the relationship you have with your money.

If you're planning on investing your surplus income, does this mean you'll have less to put into your savings? How will this impact your day-to-day life?

Sending your surplus income to an investment may increase your rate of return, and give you a future income stream, however, you're now sitting with more risk – how do you feel about that?

When looking at all your options, be sure to consider the opportunity cost of each of the options that exist to make sure you're picking the best outcome for you and your personal situation. Use the table below to consider a few of your goals and weigh them up against each other.

Hot tip: This is also a great time to think back to your personal values and ethical priorities, as well.

● ●

STRATEGY PROS AND CONS

Goal 1

Strategy 1	
Pros	**Cons**

Strategy 2	
Pros	**Cons**

Strategy 3	
Pros	**Cons**

Repeat this exercise for all the goals you have.

● ●

4. Finalise your investor risk tolerance

Now you know how much you're planning to invest and you have clarity on what you're investing for, I bet you're thinking the next thing I'm going to get you to work out is *where* to invest, but hold your horses! You need to review your investor risk tolerance and have a good think about which asset classes are going to work for your particular situation.

I want you to think about investing like you do your favourite pair of jeans – it's all about getting the right fit. As mentioned previously, you won't have the same approach to investment risk as anyone else because you're beautifully unique, so it's important to find out what you're comfortable with before forming your investment strategy.

● ●

QUIZ: WHAT TYPE OF INVESTOR ARE YOU?

Circle the appropriate responses to the questions below:

1. How long would you expect to invest before you would need access to funds?

A – Very short term (the next six months)
B – Short term (the next 12–18 months)
C – Short to medium term (the next 18 months to three years)
D – Medium term (the next three to five years)
E – Medium to long term (the next five to ten years)
F – Long term (more than ten years)

2. What type of investments have your previous (or current) investments been?

A – I only have investment experience in basic banking products and
     term deposits (i.e. never invested in bonds, shares or property).

B – I have had minimal exposure to basic banking products, as well as bonds and property.

C – I have had some investment experience and some exposure to property and equities in the past.

D – I have had some experience in all major asset classes, including Australian shares as well as some minimal experience with international shares.

E – I have had a lot of experience in all asset classes, with particular focus on Australian and international shares.

F – I have had a great deal of experience in all asset classes, including the overseas share markets and 'exotic' investment products, such as artwork or luxury cars.

3. Which of the following best describes your investment objectives?

A – To generate an income without reinvesting dividends.

B – To generate an income and a small amount of growth.

C – To generate an equal amount of income and growth.

D – To generate a small amount of income and to have substantial growth.

E – To generate growth with little to no income.

F – To generate growth with no income. (This means you're constantly reinvesting your dividends to take full advantage of compound interest so you're left with the biggest possible income at retirement.)

4. If your investment strategy was for the long term (minimum seven to ten years), how would you react if in six months' time, your portfolio decreased in value by 20 per cent?

A – I would not accept any declines in the value of my investment portfolio.

B – I would transfer my investments to more stable investment markets.

C – I would be somewhat concerned, but can accept very short-term volatility in the markets.

D – I would adopt a 'wait and see' approach to see if the
    investments improve before making a decision.

E – I know the risks and volatility levels are higher, so I would leave
    the original long-term strategy in place to let it run its course.

F – As I expect long-term growth, I would intend on investing more
    money to take advantage of the lower average investment
    prices.

**5. In consideration of your investment objectives and the level of
volatility you could tolerate, hypothetically which of the below
annual return scenarios (with a ten-year compound return) would
you feel most comfortable with over the long-term?**

	Year 1	Year 2	Year 3	Year 5	Year 7	Year 10
A	2.4% pa	4.1% pa	3.5% pa	3.0% pa	2.5% pa	2.9% pa
B	4.0% pa	4.5% pa	3.8% pa	4.0% pa	5.0% pa	4.1% pa
C	5.0% pa	4.8% pa	5.2% pa	5.9% pa	6.1% pa	5.4% pa
D	6.9% pa	2.0% pa	9.9% pa	5.2% pa	-2.9% pa	6.8% pa
E	-2.8% pa	4.5% pa	11.5% pa	8.2% pa	-5.5% pa	7.9% pa
F	9.4% pa	-3.7% pa	14.8% pa	-13.0% pa	10.5% pa	9.1% pa

Results: add up your score by writing the number of times you
ticked each letter.

A	B	C	D	E	F

If you mostly selected . . .

A - You're defensive

Type A investors associate the term 'risk' with high danger. When you make a financial decision, you may tend to focus on possible losses instead of possible long-term gains. Since you only seek basic returns and would like a low level of risk without growth, you might consider investing in fixed interest products for one to three years.

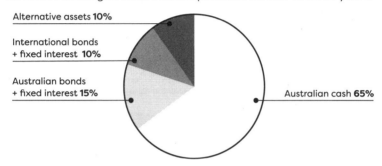

Alternative assets **10%**

International bonds
+ fixed interest **10%**

Australian bonds
+ fixed interest **15%**

Australian cash **65%**

B - You're a conservative

Type B investors only have a basic understanding of investments. Your main goal is protecting your capital, which is why you seek moderate returns and do not wish to take on more than a low level of risk. You might consider an investment time frame of three to five years, and structure your portfolio to have 70 per cent defensive assets and 30 per cent growth assets.

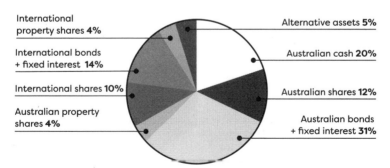

International
property shares **4%**

International bonds
+ fixed interest **14%**

International shares **10%**

Australian property
shares **4%**

Alternative assets **5%**

Australian cash **20%**

Australian shares **12%**

Australian bonds
+ fixed interest **31%**

C – You're a moderate conservative

Type C investors have a general understanding of investments, but wish to have a broader understanding so they can explore more options. You are mostly focused on possible losses, but still optimistic of gains. Aware that some volatility is to be expected, you may consider an investment time frame of three to five years and structure your portfolio to have 50 per cent defensive assets and 50 per cent growth assets.

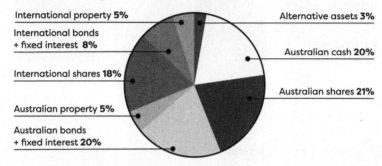

International property **5%**
International bonds + fixed interest **8%**
International shares **18%**
Australian property **5%**
Australian bonds + fixed interest **20%**
Alternative assets **3%**
Australian cash **20%**
Australian shares **21%**

D – You're a moderate grower

Type D investors are all about diverse portfolios that protect them from inflation and tax. With a reasonable understanding of investments, you are more likely to focus on possible gains, but are still mindful of risk. You may consider an investment time frame of five to seven years, and structure your portfolio to have 30 per cent defensive assets and 70 per cent growth assets.

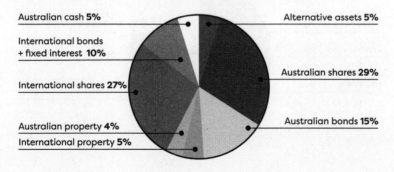

Australian cash **5%**
International bonds + fixed interest **10%**
International shares **27%**
Australian property **4%**
International property **5%**
Alternative assets **5%**
Australian shares **29%**
Australian bonds **15%**

E – You're a growth investor

Type E investors are grow-getters! (See what I did there?) With a firm understanding of investments, you associate risk with opportunity. Because your goal is to see your capital grow, you may consider an investment time frame of seven years or more, and structure your portfolio to have 15 per cent defensive assets and 85 per cent growth assets.

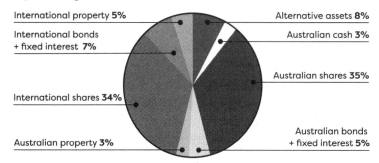

International property **5%**

International bonds + fixed interest **7%**

International shares **34%**

Australian property **3%**

Alternative assets **8%**

Australian cash **3%**

Australian shares **35%**

Australian bonds + fixed interest **5%**

F – You're a high-growth investor!

Type F investors are in it for the long run. You are aggressive when it comes to reinvesting dividends because your aim is to grow a portfolio that delivers a substantial income at the time of retirement. Because you tend to focus on possible gains and equate risk with thrill, you may consider an investment time frame of ten or more years and structure your portfolio to have 100 per cent growth assets.

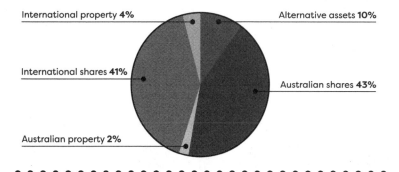

International property **4%**

International shares **41%**

Australian property **2%**

Alternative assets **10%**

Australian shares **43%**

It's down to you

Deciding where and how you'd like to invest your money ultimately comes down to your values and personal financial situation.

I always, *always* recommend speaking to a financial adviser, because they're going to give you a customised strategy that puts you in the best position to achieve your personal goals.

You also need to make sure that you have the correct lifestyle mindset to invest. This means maintaining good cash flow and saving habits so that you are able to contribute to your investment plan on a consistent basis.

5. Choosing what to invest in

This step is often the most daunting to take, but it doesn't need to be. Picking where to invest is much easier after you've got all the semantics of why, what and when worked out.

In Australia, there are a plethora of different options when it comes to what you can invest in and we've already discussed (nearly!) them all. Now's the time for you to pick what to invest in. While it might feel intimidating, remember you now have all the tools and resources you need to select what aligns most closely to your beliefs and values.

You know what funds you're starting with, the level of return you're hoping for, and the type of risk you're taking on, so the choices have very likely been whittled down to only a couple that you'd be comfortable with. It's safe to assume that if you came out as a conservative investor, for example, you're not about to run straight into a portfolio of exotic investments!

When choosing what to invest in, you're going to want to refer back to your risk profile and the suggested asset allocation that sits alongside your profile. Asset allocation means dividing your investment into a number of different investments, each representing a percentage as a whole.

If you've come out as a conservative investor, you might consider putting half your investment into shares and the other half into a fixed interest asset. If you wanted to create more diversification, you might add additional asset classes to the list, such as a greater number of shares. It doesn't need to be overwhelming; just take it step by step.

If you've skipped ahead to here . . . sorry! There simply aren't any quick answers or silver platters. This is important work that needs to be done – by you.

To work out what asset allocation strategy is best for you, it is essential that you understand your risk tolerance. If the idea of owning international shares that can fluctuate a lot keeps you tossing and turning every night, maybe you want to consider something with lower risk, like bonds or fixed interest. Nothing in investing ever needs to be an all-or-nothing decision; even the most pro-risk investors need to ensure they have diversification to put themselves in the best possible position.

DIVERSIFICATION

I've mentioned it a few times but if you're not totally sure what I mean when I say diversification, it's basically the opposite of putting all your eggs in one basket. You spread them out across multiple baskets instead! In more literal terms, you diversify by investing your money across different asset classes. It's an investment strategy that helps to spread your portfolio's risk (because you're limiting your exposure to any one type of asset) and increase the likelihood of more stable returns.

Diversification is key, and it's important to also know that when we diversify, we aren't only doing it to manage risk (although sometimes it feels that way!). When we diversify, we can actually reap greater rewards from our portfolios.

Nobel Prize-winning economist Harry Markowitz reportedly referred to this reward as 'the only free lunch in finance'. Basically, you are likely to earn more if you diversify your portfolio.

Here's an example to help illustrate what Markowitz was talking about:

- If you'd invested $100 in the S&P 500 in 1970 it would have grown to $7,771 by the end of 2013.
- Investing the same amount over the same period in commodities, such as the benchmark S&P GSCI Index, would have made your money grow to $4,829.
- If, however, you'd split your $100 in half and invested $50 in the S&P 500 and the other $50 in the S&P GSCI, your total investment would have grown to $9,457 over the same period.[33]

So, when we compare all three, your return in the third, diversified scenario would have surpassed the S&P 500-only portfolio by 20 per cent and be almost double that of the S&P GSCI performance. Not an insignificant difference! This is an example of exactly why a blended approach tends to work better.

DIVERSIFIED

$100 IN S&P 500
1970–2013
$7,771

$100 IN COMMODITIES
1970–2013
$4,829

$50 IN S&P 500
$50 IN S&P GSCI
1970–2013
$9,457

You might like to flick back to the pie chart corresponding to your investor risk tolerance earlier in this chapter for an example of what diversification can look like.

6. Choosing how to invest

Investment platforms act as a place to buy, sell and hold all your investments. Which one to use is one of the most popular questions I get asked. I have an inkling that it's because none of us love the idea of commitment, and that's what it feels like you're doing when you pick an investment platform.

Unfortunately (like so many other investment-related questions!), I'm not able to answer where the best place to invest is for your personal circumstances.

Not because I don't want to – I'd love to be able to say which platform is best for you, that'd make everyone's life easy! – but because there isn't one 'best' platform out there. When looking at an investment platform, you're not only looking at fees; you're looking at all the other features and benefits that platform offers and the platform's capabilities. Don't be fooled into thinking they're all the same!

If you're looking for a micro-investing platform because that's what suits you and your life stage right now, looking at a platform that has a high entry point and needs you to stump up $1,000 a month to stay involved isn't going to work – and it can make you feel overwhelmed. Instead, work out what features are important to you.

Are you looking for a cool app to track your investments really easily? Are you looking at accessing direct shares? Or are you actually wanting to get a robo-advice platform that'll make the decisions for you?

All of these needs will have a different platform that will be more or less suitable, and it's up to you to weigh the benefits and what works best for you. To make things as easy as possible for you, here are five things I'd recommend you consider when picking an investing platform:

Fees

All platforms will have some kind of associated fee. If they say they're fee-free, I want you to do a deep dive into their product disclosure statement (PDS) and find out how they're making money, because in the investment world, nobody does anything for free.

Each investment platform charges in a different way, so it can be challenging to compare apples with apples. Some will have a monthly fee while others might only charge brokerage when you buy or sell an asset. Some platforms charge flat fees and others a percentage, so choosing one that is right for you is going to depend on how much you're investing to begin with, and what your ongoing contributions look like.

Pick one that works for you – and try not to always focus on which is the cheapest because, as I've said before, if you pay peanuts, you might get monkeys.

What are you investing in?

This one's important, as some platforms have limited access. Are you looking for direct shares, ETFs, a managed fund, or a bond? All are available on platforms, but not all are available on every platform, so working out what asset you're purchasing before looking at the platform you're going to buy it on is important. Take extra care when picking a platform if your plan is to invest in a number of asset classes, because you'll want to try to avoid having to use multiple platforms and doubling up on fees.

Do you need help?

Hopefully you're feeling incredibly empowered, but you might still feel like you've got analysis paralysis, especially if you're trying to invest a large amount of money, or you've gotten this far and realised that as much as you want to invest, you just don't have any interest in it.

Most platforms don't offer independent investment advice (except for robo-advice platforms!) and if you're finding yourself looking for a hand to hold, maybe looking into a less automated solution or having a chat with a qualified financial adviser is the go. In my first book, I outlined all the things I recommend looking for when you're seeking a financial adviser, so you might like to refer back to that.

Contact

If you're investing your life savings on a platform, I'm assuming you want good customer service – because I would! This goes back to my pay peanuts, might get monkeys comment – many platforms that pride themselves on a high standard of customer service do have to charge a bit of a premium for that, so you'll pay for the privilege, and also have to make sure you're getting what you're paying for.

Access and useability

There's no point picking a platform you don't know how to use or access. Some of you might prioritise a nice app where you can track your investments in one click on your morning commute. Others might like a more comprehensive platform that has oodles of research and data to take into consideration.

Make sure you're picking a platform that fits into your life and isn't out of sight, out of mind.

In the following table I've pulled together some top-line info for you about various different trading and advisory platforms, based on their offering at the time of writing. This is just an overview and I definitely encourage you to supplement it with your own research, but I hope it helps you with the all-important compare-and-contrast if you plan to feature shares in your portfolio. Go forth and make your selection – you've got this!

Platform	Description	Fees	AU shares?	US shares?	ETFs?	CHESS sponsorship?	Round-up feature?	Minimum investment amount	Additional information
Commsec	Trading platform	0.12% (over $25,000)	✓	✓	✓	✓		$500	Includes New York and London Stock Exchanges
Commsec Pocket	Seven ETF investment options	No account-keeping fees. ETF management fee varies from 0.09% to 0.67% of your investment per year depending on the ETF. $2 per trade up to $1000 and 20c on trades over $1000			✓			$50	
eToro	Trading platform	All withdrawal fees are subject to a US$5 fee. Inactivity fee of US$10 charged monthly after 12 months of no login activity. Conversion fees for wires and other payment methods apply.		✓	✓			$10	Also has access to crypto
Pearler	Both a share trading platform and a micro-investing platform with eight ETF portfolio options	Micro-investing: $1.70 per month for one fund or $2.30 per month for multiple funds. No fees charged on balances under $100. Regular investing: $6.50 per transaction + 0.5% per foreign exchange conversion between AU$ and US$	✓	✓	✓	✓	✓ For micro-investing	$100	

	Type	Fees					Minimum	Notes
Raiz	Micro-investing with seven ETF portfolio options	Standard portfolios: $3.50 per month for accounts under $15,000 and 0.275% per year for accounts over $15,000 Custom portfolio: $4.50 per month for accounts under $20,000 and 0.275% per year for accounts over $20,000 Sapphire portfolio: $3.50 per month and 0.275% per year				✓	$5	
Selfwealth	Trading platform	$9.50 brokerage regardless of trade size on AU and US shares	✓	✓	✓		$500	Includes access to extensive research and analytics
Sharesies	Trading platform	0.5% for amounts up to $3000 and 0.1% for amounts above $3000. 0.4% currency exchange fee when you exchange money	✓	✓	✓		$0	Also has access to the New Zealand Exchange
Six Park*	Robo advisory platform	0.66% per year for amounts between $10,000 and $200,000 0.528% per year for amounts between $200,000 and $2,000,000 0.395% per year for amounts over $2,000,000		✓	✓		$2000	Investment decisions are made by Six Park's investment advisory committee

Investment platform table

Platform	Type					Minimum	Notes
Spaceship	Micro-investing with three managed fund options				✓	$0	
Stake	Trading platform: $3 brokerage for AU shares and $0 brokerage for US shares	✓	✓	✓		$500	
Stockspot	Robo advisory platform: $6.25 per month for amounts between $2000 and $4999; $9.95 per month for amounts between $5,000 and $19,999; 0.5% per year for amounts between $20,000 and $199,999; 0.4% per year for amounts between $200,000 and $499,999; 0.3% for amounts over $500,000		✓	✓		$2000	All investment decisions are made by an algorithm
Superhero	Trading platform: $5 brokerage on AU shares and $0 brokerage on US shares and Australian ETFs	✓	✓			$100	You can earn Qantas points on eligible trades and transfers

Note: information current as at June 2022.

*Disclaimer: Six Park is the asset management company that powers the She's on the Money online investment service. Please also note that Superhero and Sharesies have worked with She's on the Money in an advertising capacity; however, this has not influenced the information presented.

7. Implement your investment plan

This is the fun bit, or at least I find it super fun!

By now, you've done 99 per cent of the work to create your investment plan, so it's time to pull it together and get it implemented.

So far, you've looked at your personal situation, you know what you can invest, you've set goals, done your pros and cons, and picked assets and platforms that work for you.

It's a good idea to write a to-do list of the tasks required to get started. This might include things like registering for platforms, setting up direct debits, finding the fun or celebrating the milestones. This will help you work through the relevant tasks one by one until it's all set up.

As you pull together everything (I suggest doing this in Word or a Googledoc, so everything is in one place and easy to review), it's important to really keep the bigger picture in mind. Having gone through all your options for reaching your goals and weighed up each strategy, it's not going to be simple to get this down on paper.

Finalising your plan ensures you're making decisions as to which goal you'll start working towards first, and what's really achievable for you.

Your journey is going to be so much easier to take once you have it all mapped out. If everything is feeling a bit much, don't worry! All we need to do is break down your goals into smaller, more palatable steps.

If, for example, your goal is to invest $10,000 in the next two years, that might feel overwhelming, especially if you've never done it before – so break it down!

$10,000 over two years → $5,000 each year.
$5,000 a year → $417 each month.
$417 each month → $96 a week.
$96 a week → $14 a day.

Does that feel a bit more achievable?

These concrete steps you're creating for yourself are going to become the framework for your future, and that's so exciting. You're an investor now; who would have thought?!

If you find yourself falling off track, don't be hard on yourself. Everyone does that – even I do that (more often than I'd like to admit). What we need to do is always be willing to get back up and try again.

Those who are successful aren't the ones who were handed a golden ticket (just look at what happens to people when they win the lottery!). Success comes to those who get up when they're knocked down, wipe off the dust and try again.

I know you can do this. You're tenacious, and I'm so proud of you.

8. Review and rebalance

SURPRISE! I bet you thought I was done with you ... but not yet. This final, and slightly less exciting, step is arguably the most important of all.

You might have done all your due diligence at each step along the way to creating your investment plan. You might have done absolutely everything to dot all your i's and cross all your t's – but life is messy and beautiful and ever-changing, and so is your investment plan.

For this reason, we have to review our plan regularly, and always look back over it when things change. Put in a diary prompt to remind yourself every quarter, six months or year to check in and review your strategy. There will also be life events that prompt you to review. For instance ...

Got a pay rise? Review time.

Got a new partner? Review time.

Pets? Review time.

Babies? *Definitely* review time.

You get the picture.

Reviewing your investment plan every few months or so is going to help you ensure you're always on track to meeting your goals. Original strategies might not be relevant now. You might have achieved a goal or you might have had something big pop up that's a more urgent priority.

Reviewing and rebalancing (as I explained in Chapter 12) regularly is going to keep you on track, and that's where we want to be. Because no matter how perfect you get your investment plan, or how detailed the plan is, one thing is guaranteed to happen: life.

Your financial situation might change, or even your values might change. You might have unexpected expenses, or you might change your priorities. All of these are valid and all of these are exciting, but all need to be considered.

As I said before, you can't set-and-forget – it's not an option – so commit to reassessing your situation regularly. It's one of the best things you can do for Future You.

• • • • • •

And there you have it, my friend – an entire book that takes you through the ins and outs of investing, because you asked for it. This book was written by me for you. Historically, the investing space hasn't included women in its conversations, and once we were included, often there was an assumption that we needed to be coaxed into understanding the space. The media has also discouraged our involvement: a decent proportion of their financial content propagates stereotypes about women and money. Headlines feature either women with shopping addictions or risk-averse women making the grocery budget stretch. These stereotypes aren't who we are! Research tells us we're actually great investors who outperform men when it comes to portfolio returns.[34]

So, let's take our power back and invest like women. Being a woman is incredibly powerful, and when we have strong financial literacy the entire world becomes a better place. We are becoming more confident and starting to hold more space in the investment world, and for good reason. Not only are we making great decisions but we're talking about them and we're sharing them through our friendship circles and communities such as She's on the Money. We're countering the idea that finance is a man's game.

I'm so incredibly proud of you taking this step towards creating financial freedom for yourself, and super grateful that I get to play a very small part in your journey towards it. You are powerful beyond belief, and remember that the first step is always the hardest to take, but you've got this – and there's a whole community behind you. When one of us succeeds, all of us succeed, my friend, because a rising tide lifts all ships.

● ● ● ● ● ●

SIMONE, 26 – VIC

I have a high-risk super investment strategy, which suits me as I'm only 26. It's also a well-performing super fund, which is important to me. I make personal super contributions as my employer puts a higher percentage in if I do so. It works well for me, particularly as someone who did limited work for three years while I did my PhD. Now that I work full-time, I'm happy to see my super growing. I want to invest $22,000 in 2022, but so far I've invested nothing. I need a better regular investment strategy because I don't know what I'm waiting for. My money is in the bank, not working for me!

KIMBERLY, 24 – NSW

I haven't invested in individual shares because I feel like I don't know enough about each individual share to have a diversified portfolio on my own judgement. Rather, I opt for investing in ETFs and managed funds. I have $25 that goes into a fund every week, and I make irregular investments into another portfolio, but I haven't really grasped how I would formalise my investment strategy. I've been wanting to change my super for a while too, to one that more aligns to my values. The one I'm in isn't bad, but I definitely want to do a thorough evaluation.

● ● ● ● ● ●

TAKE NOTE

Make sure you've got the rest of your money in
great shape *before* you start investing.

....

Set your goals, track your progress – and celebrate your successes!

....

Once you've got a plan going that works for you, remember to keep
reviewing and tweaking it over time to keep it fully optimised.

....

Glossary

Accumulation fund A type of superannuation fund in which the benefit a member receives reflects total contributions as well as whatever they have earned, minus expenses and tax, so the benefit reflects the performance of the fund's investments.

Annual report The document a company uses to communicate details of activities, financial results and strategies to shareholders and other stakeholders.

ASIC The Australian Securities and Investments Commission. ASIC's role is to regulate companies and financial services and enforce laws to protect Australian consumers, investors and creditors.

ASX The Australia Stock Exchange is the location where financial products such as shares and bonds are bought and sold in Australia.

Australian Taxation Office (ATO) The Australian government's principal revenue collection agency.

Bad debt Debt that does not contribute to future wealth creation or furthering your education. Bad debt is most often any type of debt that you won't be able to claim on tax, and you haven't used to purchase an asset that increases in value. Personally, I categorise personal loans, credit cards and car loans as bad debt.

Balance sheet A statement of a company's assets and liabilities through a specific period, detailing income and spending in that time.

Bear market A bear market is defined as a market which, in a period of at least two months, falls by 20 per cent or more.

Behavioural finance What really drives investment markets. Kind of a marriage between psychology and finance, which attempts to explain how humans make financial decisions in real life and why their decisions might not appear to be rational every time. For example, many people will sell shares in a falling market when that is a time of opportunity, and logic would suggest that during a falling market is when you should be purchasing. Smart investors keep their feelings in check. As the great Warren Buffett says, be fearful when others are greedy, and greedy when others are fearful.

Bond A bond is a fixed income asset that represents a loan made by an investor to a borrower. Bonds are issued by governments and corporations when they want to raise money. When you invest in a bond, you're lending money to a company or the government and the bond pays interest at regular intervals.

Broker An authorised buyer who acts on behalf of a group of people, a company or an individual.

Budget A budget is an epic tool to create a plan for your money. A budget is not like a diet – it's a tool to ensure that every dollar that comes into your bank account is put to work. A budget isn't a guesstimate, it's what you're really spending. When you create a budget you need to be honest with yourself about your spending habits.

Bull market A bull market is defined as a market which rises by around 20 per cent over two months or more.

Capital The cost of your investment, or the initial starting funds.

Capital gains tax (CGT) Tax due and payable when an investment is sold if it is sold for more than what you initially purchased it for. The gain is added to your taxable income on your tax return.

Cash A highly secure asset class that is usually great where liquidity is key.

Cash flow For an individual, cash flow is the difference between how much money you have coming into your bank account each month, and how much you have going out. For a company, it refers to the net amount of cash being transferred into and out of the company, usually over a 12-month period.

Cognitive bias A thought process that filters the information around us through the prism of personal experience or what we ourselves prefer to do or see.

Compound interest Compound interest is the eighth wonder of the modern world. It is the interest earned on money that was previously earned as interest. It causes your money to compound over time. It's brilliant for savings and investments, but can work against you if you're paying interest on a loan. Frequency, time, the interest rate, and your starting amount all make compound interest powerful. If you understand it properly, you'll earn it. If you don't, you might end up paying it.

Concessional contribution A concessional superannuation contribution is a payment made into your super fund from your before-tax income. This includes your superannuation guarantee contributions. Concessional contributions are taxed at 15 per cent when they are received by your super fund. From 1 July 2022 the concessional contributions cap each year is $27,500; however, your cap might be higher if you didn't use the full amount of your cap in previous years.

Cryptocurrency A form of digital currency.

Debt consolidation Combining various debts, whether they are credit card bills or loan payments, into one monthly payment.

Diversification of investments Diversification is the practice of spreading your investments around so that your exposure to any one type of asset is limited. This practice is designed to help reduce the volatility of your portfolio over time.

Dividend The income you receive from shares, just like receiving rent on a property or interest from a bank. It is a sum of money paid regularly (typically annually) by a company to its shareholders out of its profits (or reserves).

Dollar cost averaging When you regularly contribute the same amount of money to an investment at the same time each month regardless of the price of that investment. Dollar-cost averaging can be a very effective way to manage risk when investing in assets like shares as it can in some cases take away the 'timing risk' of trying to pick the bottom of the market (which is impossible because we aren't able to accurately predict the future!).

Estate planning An estate plan is a comprehensive plan that includes documents that are effective during your lifetime as well as other documents that aren't in effect until your death.

ETF An exchange traded fund: a basket of different investments that are selected to create diversification, and provide exposure to a variety of assets, including stocks, bonds and commodities.

Family trust A common type of trust used to hold assets or run a family business.

Financial adviser A person whose job is to provide financial advice to clients.

Financial freedom Financial freedom is the point at which you no longer have to go to work to create an income and have created investments that pay you a passive income so you've got the freedom of choice without the worry of needing to financially sustain your lifestyle.

Financial planner A qualified financial adviser who gives clients a broad range of advice – for example, on investing (me, here!), tax, super and retirement, and estate planning.

Fixed interest A secure asset class which usually refers to bonds. It's relatively secure if you lend to financially stable companies or the Australian government.

Franking credits Franking credits are a form of tax credit paid by a company to shareholders when it pays out dividends. Because the company has already paid tax on the dividends, giving out a franking credit means that it is essentially giving a tax credit to its shareholders.

Good debt Debt which contributes to wealth creation or furthering your education. Good debt can be a home loan, or an investment loan.

HECS-HELP debt The Higher Education Contribution Scheme-Higher Education Loan Program is a scheme that assists eligible Commonwealth-supported students to pay their student contribution amount with a loan. HECS-HELP loans are available at all public universities and at a handful of private higher education providers.

Home loan A home loan or mortgage is a loan advanced to you by a financial institution in return for security over the property you are using the loan to buy.

Income protection insurance An insurance designed to pay you a benefit if you are unable to work for a period of time because of illness or injury. Income protection allows you to protect your largest asset – your ability to work and produce an income! An income protection policy can pay up to 75 per cent of your pre-tax income for a set period of time.

Income statement A statement that shows the company's revenues, costs and expenses over a particular time span, and its resulting profit or loss. It's sometimes referred to as a 'profit and loss statement'.

Index fund An index fund is a portfolio of shares or bonds designed to mimic the composition and performance of a financial market index.

Indexation Indexation means adjusting a price, wage, or other value based on the changes in another price or composite indicator of prices. Indexation can be done to adjust for the effects of inflation, cost of living, or input prices over time, or to adjust for different prices and costs in different geographic areas.

Inheritance Inheritance refers to the assets that an individual leaves to his or her loved ones after he or she passes away. An inheritance may contain cash, investments such as stocks or bonds, and other assets such as jewellery, cars and real estate.

Interest Money paid regularly at a particular rate for the use of money lent, or for delaying the repayment of a debt.

IPO An initial public offering; i.e. the first time that the shares of a previously private company are offered for sale to members of the public on the stock exchange.

Lenders mortgage insurance LMI is a one-off, non-refundable premium that can be paid upfront to the lending institution or added to your home loan when you don't have a whole 20 per cent deposit or a guarantor. The purpose of LMI is to protect the lender in the event that you default on your home loan, by reducing the risk to the lender – not to protect you as a lender.

Life insurance Typically, life insurance is an agreement that if you die, or are diagnosed with a terminal illness, a sum of money will be paid out to (typically) your spouse or children. You can also have this death benefit paid to other members in your family.

Lifestyle creep Something that happens to the best of us! Lifestyle creep occurs when your income increases and former luxuries become new necessities. For example, when I was at uni I would buy make-up at the supermarket, and now that I've got a full-time job I purchase all my cosmetics from Adore Beauty.

Liquidity How easy it is to convert your investment back into cash by selling it. For example, the liquidity of a share is approximately three days to sell and the cash be back in your bank account, but when you sell a house that asset could take more than three months to land cash in your pocket.

Maternity and parental leave Leave from work granted to a parent before and after the birth of their child. In Australia we have Parental Leave Pay, which is a payment for up to 18 weeks while you care for your new child and is based on the weekly rate of the national minimum wage.

Money story Your money story is a very personal narrative about money that started to form in childhood. Your money story makes up your thoughts, feeling and beliefs about money and deeply affects your ability to make financial decisions. You can't choose the money story you're born with, but you can choose to change your course now.

moneysmart.gov.au A government website with plenty of fantastic resources to further your financial education, which I absolutely adore because it's a destination that carries no bias.

Negative gearing Where the rental income you receive on a property you own is less than the interest payments and expenses you incur each year, meaning the property costs you money each year to own.

Neutral gearing Where the rental income you receive on a property you own is equal to the interest payments and expenses you incur each year, meaning the property breaks even each year.

Non-concessional contributions (NCCs) Money you put into your super using your 'after-tax' dollars or your personal savings. These are personal contributions that you make into your own super account that are not claimed as a tax deduction. From 1 July 2021 the non-concessional contributions cap (the most amount of money you can put into your super) is $110,000, meaning if you put more into your super you'll have to pay additional tax.

Offset account A transaction account that is directly linked to your home loan.

Okay debt Okay debt is debt that isn't as bad as 'bad debt', although you don't want to have it for the long term, but it's debt you've used to either purchase assets that increase in value, or debts that you can claim on tax. An example of okay debt is your HECS-HELP loan, where you don't accrue interest and you've used it to further educate yourself so you can increase your income in the future.

Performance fee A performance fee is a payment made to an investment manager for generating positive returns. Performance fees don't exist on all investments but are definitely something to understand.

Personal loan A loan which allows you to borrow a specific amount of money, usually from a financial institution, and then repay the debt with interest in equal payments over an agreed term.

Portfolio A collection of financial products. For example, your investment portfolio might include property, bonds, shares and more.

Positive gearing Where the rental income you receive on a property you own is more than the interest payments and expenses you incur each year, meaning the property makes you money each year.

Returns The amount you make or lose on your investment. This can be expressed in dollars or as a percentage.

Revenue This is sometimes known as the top line. It's the money a company has received as a result of its operations, usually the proceeds of sales.

Risk In investment terms, it is the probability of the price going up and down, and therefore the likelihood of you losing money or making returns.

Salary sacrifice An arrangement between an employer and an employee, where the employee agrees to forgo part of their future entitlement to salary or wages. This is in return for the employer providing them with benefits of a similar value.

Savings account A savings account is an interest-bearing deposit account held at a bank or other financial institution. Your savings accounts shouldn't have fees and if they do you need to change that, pronto!

Self-managed super fund (SMSF) A private super fund that you manage yourself. Typically I would only ever suggest an SMSF if you are very interested in managing your super more actively and have a minimum of $600,000 in your account.

Share Sometimes referred to as a stock or security, a share is a unit of ownership in a company. If you buy a share in a company, you own a part or a 'share' of that company. This part ownership is sometimes referred to as holding equity. As a shareholder you generally have certain entitlements, like receiving a portion of the profits that company generates and being able to sell that share at a profit if the company increases in value.

Share market The share market (some fancy pants people like to call it the stock exchange) is a transparent and regulated marketplace in which shares in public companies are bought and sold. Here in Australia we have a national share market – the ASX, or the Australian Securities Exchange.

Shareholder Any person who owns shares (that's me and possibly you too – if not already, then soon!)

Speculative share A share that carries a really high level of risk, with the possibility of a high rate of return.

Stock Tends to be used interchangeably with share, but where share always refers to an individual unit, stock can mean a portion of those units. You'd say 'Stock in Telstra rose today,' but 'My shares in Telstra rose today.'

Superannuation Superannuation is NOT an investment; it is a tax structure. Also known as 'super', it is a way of investing money while you are working and earning an income, so that you will have an income when you retire. As of 1 July 2022, employers need to pay into an eligible employee's super fund regardless of the employee's rate of pay. (Employees under 18 have to work more than 30 hours in a week to be eligible.) Take superannuation seriously now, as one day it is very likely going to be your largest asset class.

Superannuation guarantee (SG) This is a percentage of your salary set by the government that your employer pays to your superannuation fund. If you're an employee, you might see SG on your pay slip. At the time of writing, the rate for SG payments by an employer is 10.5 per cent of your salary.

Term deposit A term deposit is a cash investment held at a financial institution. Your money is invested for an agreed rate of interest over a fixed amount of time, or term.

Trade The action of buying and selling of stocks.

Undervalued share A share that has been assessed or valued as being worth less than it should be.

Volatility This is how much the price of an asset fluctuates over time.

Will A legal document that exists to direct what happens to your assets when you pass away. A will gives you the ability to express exactly how you would like your assets distributed and what happens to any children (or pets!), instead of letting the law decide for you. According to ASIC, approximately half of all Australians die without a will.

Notes

1   Anastasia Anagnostakos, 'Closing the gap – the rise of female share investors', ASX, 5 March 2021, 2.asx.com.au/blog/investor-update/2021/closing-the-gap-the-rise-of-female-share-investors

2   Maurie Backman, 'Women and Investing: 20 Years of Research and Statistics Summarized', The Motley Fool, 9 March 2022, fool.com/research/women-in-investing-research/

3   Kathleen Riach, Colin O'Hare, Barbara Dalton and Chelle Wang, 'The Future Face of Poverty is Female: Stories Behind Australian Women's Superannuation Poverty in Retirement', AustralianSuper, 2018, australiansuper.com/campaigns/future-face-of-poverty

4   'ASFA retirement standard', superannuation.asn.au/resources/retirement-standard

5   Workplace Gender Equality Agency, 'Women's economic security in retirement: insight paper', February 2020, wgea.gov.au/sites/default/files/documents/Women%27s_economic_security_in_retirement.pdf

6   Mary King, Malin Ortenblad, and Jamie J. Ladge, 'What Will It Take to Make Finance More Gender-Balanced?', *Harvard Business Review*, 10 December 2018, hbr.org/2018/12/what-will-it-take-to-make-finance-more-gender-balanced

7   Dr Kathleen Gurney, *Your Money Personality: What It Is and How You Can Profit From It*, Financial Psychology Corporation, Ohio, 1988

8   Beth Kobliner, 'Money habits are set by age 7. Teach your kids the value of a dollar now', PBS, 5 April 2018, pbs.org/newshour/economy/making-sense/money-habits-are-set-by-age-7-teach-your-kids-the-value-of-a-dollar-now

9   Warren Buffett, 'Buy American. I Am', *New York Times*, 16 October 2008, nytimes.com/2008/10/17/opinion/17buffett.html

10   ASX, 'Issuer code allocation', 2015, asx.com.au/documents/resources/ASX_Issuer_Code_Allocation.pdf

11   Vanguard digital index chart, insights.vanguard.com.au/VolatilityIndexChart/ui/advisor.html

12   'How Much Would Apple Stock Be Worth If It Never Split?', Investopedia, investopedia.com/articles/stocks/12/history-apple-stock-increases.asp#toc-how-much-would-apple-stock-be-worth-if-it-never-split

13   'Robo Advisory Market Predicted to Gather a Revenue of $59,344.5 Million by 2028, Growing at a Healthy CAGR of 39.9% from 2021-2028', PR Newswire, 16 June 2022, au.finance.yahoo.com/news/robo-advisory-market-predicted-gather-125000519.html

14   Property Pulse, 'Peak, peaking, peaked,' CoreLogic, 7 March 2022, corelogic.com.au/news-research/news/archive/peak,-peaking,-peaked-how-to-read-australias-housing-market

15   '25 Years of Housing Trends', CoreLogic, 2018, aussie.com.au/content/dam/aussie/documents/home-loans/aussie_25_years_report.pdf

16   Price Waterhouse Coopers, 'Beyond compliance: Consumers and employees want business to do more on ESG', Consumer Intelligence Services, 2021, pwc.com/us/en/services/consulting/library/consumer-intelligence-series/consumer-and-employee-esg-expectations.html

17   Alex Gluyas, 'Ethical investments surge past $1 trillion mark', *Australian Financial Review*, 2 September 2021, afr.com/markets/equity-markets/ethical-investments-surge-past-1-trillion-mark-20210902-p58o31

18   Morgan Stanley, 'Sustainable Services Outperform Peers in 2020 During Coronavirus', www.morganstanley.com/ideas/esg-funds-outperform-peers-coronavirus

19   Natasha White and Lisa Pham, 'ESG Funds Resist Worst of Downturn But Investors Are Spooked', Bloomberg, 19 June 2022, bloomberg.com/

news/articles/2022-06-18/esg-funds-are-losing-less-in-the-market-slump-so-far

20 Responsible Returns, 'Want to grow your money responsibly?', 2022, responsiblereturns.com.au

21 Australian Institute of Health and Welfare, 'Deaths in Australia', 9 June 2022, Australian Government, aihw.gov.au/reports/life-expectancy-death/deaths-in-australia/contents/life-expectancy (accessed 17 July 2022)

22 Emily Willingham, 'Humans Could Live up to 150 Years, New Research Suggests', Scientific American, 25 May 2021, scientificamerican.com/article/humans-could-live-up-to-150-years-new-research-suggests/

23 Australian Taxation Office, 'YourSuper Comparison Tool', Australian Government, ato.gov.au/Calculators-and-tools/YourSuper-comparison-tool/

24 KPMG, 'The Gender Superannuation Gap', report, August 2021, home.kpmg/au/en/home/insights/2021/08/gender-superannuation-gap.html

25 Jason Fernando, 'Balance Sheet', Investopedia, 5 July 2022, investopedia.com/terms/b/balancesheet.asp (accessed 18 July 2022)

26 Jason Morris, 'How do I read and analyze an income statement?', Investopedia, 7 May 2021, investopedia.com/ask/answers/100715/how-do-i-read-and-analyze-income-statement.asp (accessed 18 July 2022)

27 'What is a good return on assets', Omni calculator, omnicalculator.com/finance/roa#what-is-a-good-return-on-assets

28 My Accounting Course, 'Return on Equity (ROE) Ratio', myaccountingcourse.com/financial-ratios/return-on-equity

29 Adam Hayes, 'Interest Coverage Ratio', Investopedia, 17 June 2022, investopedia.com/terms/i/interestcoverageratio.asp (accessed 18 July 2022)

30 Troy Segal, 'What is Fundamental Market Analysis', Investopedia, September 2021, investopedia.com/terms/f/fundamentalanalysis.asp (accessed 18 July 2022)

31 ASX, 'Sharemarket game: learn about the sharemarket and how it works', 2.asx.com.au/investors/investment-tools-and-resources/sharemarket-game

32 Vanguard, 'The Power of Perspective', Vanguard Index Chart, 2021, intl.assets.vgdynamic.info/intl/australia/documents/resources/index_chart2021.pdf

33 Ben Taylor, 'How to pick your investments', Investopedia, 15 June 2021, investopedia.com/investing/how-pick-your-investments/ (accessed 25 July 2022)

34 Meghan Railey, 'If female investors have any weakness, it's their mistaken belief that they're not good investors', CNBC, 11 April 2022, cnbc.com/2022/04/11/op-ed-heres-why-women-are-better-investors-than-men.html

Acknowledgements

I can't quite believe that I'm sitting here writing the acknowledgements for my second book. As much as it's been challenging, writing this has also been one of the best experiences of my life.

I'd like to extend my most heartfelt thanks to a handful of people who've made it all possible: without you, this book would not have become a reality.

Firstly, as always, to my beautiful parents, Eric and Judi Devine. You champion and support everything I do and I am forever grateful for all you've taught me. There has not been a moment in my life when I've questioned whether or not you had my back, and I wish everyone could experience the love you shower Alex and me with.

To my fiancé, Stephen. I can't wait to write my third book and address you as my husband! You are my favourite person. You are generous and kind, and challenge me at every opportunity to be the best version of myself. Writing this book tested me with late nights, early mornings and saying no to so many things I knew you wanted me to say yes to. Thank you for supporting me, loving me and knowing the perfect moment to place a cup of tea on my desk.

To Isabelle Yates: what can I say to the woman who makes my book dreams a reality? Your belief in She's on the Money and the power of financial literacy makes my heart sing. The time, energy and effort you put into the creation of this book are nothing short of amazing. Thank you for being a true partner, holding my hand every step of the way. It blows my mind that in just two years we've been able to achieve what we have.

And finally, to *you*! Yes, you, the delightful human reading this. I'm so proud of the journey you're on, and everything you've achieved. Remember, you're exactly where you're supposed to be, and if your journey looks different to that of others, it's beautiful because it's your own. Without you, this book wouldn't exist. Because of you, the She's on the Money community is a thriving, generous, kind and inclusive space to discuss and become better at all things money. I feel humbled to be part of it all. She's on the Money has become my life, and I wouldn't want to have it any other way. Thank you from the bottom of my heart.

She's on the Money

on the

M ney

Take charge of your
financial future
Victoria Devine
Creator of Australia's #1 finance podcast

Winner of the ABIA General Non-fiction Book of the Year 2022

**Winner of the Best Personal Finance & Investment Book of the Year
at the 2021 Business Book Awards**

Through her phenomenally popular and award-winning podcast **She's on the Money**, Victoria Devine has built an empowered and supportive community of women finding their way to financial freedom.

Honest, relatable, non-judgemental and motivating, Victoria is a financial adviser who knows what millennial life is really like and where we can get stuck with money stuff. (Did someone say 'Afterpay' . . . ?) So, to help you hit your money goals without skimping on brunch, she's put all her expert advice into this accessible guide that will set you up for a healthy and happy future.

Learn how to be more secure, independent and informed with your money – with clear steps on how to budget, clear debts, build savings, start investing, buy property and much more. And along with all the practical information, Victoria will guide you through the sometimes-tricky psychology surrounding money so you can establish the values, habits and confidence that will help you build your wealth long-term.

Just like the podcast, the book is full of real-life money stories from members of the **She's on the Money** community who candidly share their experiences, wins and lessons learned to inspire others to turn their stories around, too. And with templates and activities throughout, plus a twelve-month plan to get you started, you can immediately put Victoria's recommendations into action in your own life.

You are not alone on your financial journey, and with the money principles in this book you'll go further than you ever thought possible.